The Candlemaker's Primer

The Candlemaker's Primer

by K. Lomneth Chisholm

E. P. DUTTON & CO., INC. | New York 1973

Copyright © 1973 by K. Lomneth Chisholm

All rights reserved. Printed in the U.S.A.

First Edition

No part of this publication may be reproduced or transmitted in any form or by any means, electronic or mechanical, including photocopy, recording, or any information storage and retrieval system now known or to be invented, without permission in writing from the publisher, except by a reviewer who wishes to quote brief passages in connection with a review written for inclusion in a magazine, newspaper, or broadcast.

Published simultaneously in Canada by Clarke, Irwin & Company Limited, Toronto and Vancouver

SBN: 0-525-07308-6

Library of Congress Catalog Card Number: 72-82712

This book is dedicated
to people who like to cook
between meals.

ACKNOWLEDGMENTS:

Deep appreciation must be expressed for every student I ever taught. They, in turn, taught me much of what I know today.

Deep gratitude must also go to Harry P. Messemer, Jr., Fire Chief, Scotch Plains, N.J., who was ever ready to advise a safe procedure, and to Mrs. Messemer, who so carefully read the manuscript to make sure it was totally understandable to the beginning craftsman.

Last but not least many, many thanks to Betty and Lloyd Thomforde of the Candle Barn, Watchung, N.J. Between writing and illustrating this book, the author broke both elbows. The Thomfordes came to the rescue with hours and hours of studio time to make these illustrations possible.

Contents

1	*Candle Notes*	1
2	*Waxes and Their Formulas:* Varieties, precautions, specific types: base waxes, candle construction, base formulas, dipping; shape and color coats; problems	5
3	*Cleaning and Reclaiming Waxes:* Animal waxes, tallow, vegetable waxes; used waxes; storing	18
4	*Equipment and Molds:* Workshop, small equipment and vats, dipping equipment, decorating equipment; molds both domestic and commercial	25
5	*Wicks:* History, materials, size, preparation; flame; problems	32
6	*Color and Design:* Flame colors, wax colors, color-testing, color formulas	38
7	*Fragrances:* Introducing scents, types of scent	48

8	*Pouring Your Candles:*	50
	Pouring locations, directions, releasing from mold; glass containers, paper molds, tin can molds, kitchen molds, squeaky-toy molds, bottles, spheres	
9	*Dipping Techniques:*	79
	Tapers and cylinders, sockets, swirls, color patterns, rolled texture, color dipping	
10	*Candle-Crafting:*	92
	Sheet wax, floating candles, twists, sandwich candles, burning bushes, froth, sand casting, graduated stacked candles, fireplace candles, sculpturing, hobnail patterns, reviving decorations, leftovers: granules, appliqué	
11	*The $20.00 Professional:*	118
	Sell your creations? Why not?	
	Glossary	124
	Index	127

The Candlemaker's Primer

1

Candle Notes

The contents of this book are offered to the beginning craftsman to provide quick, simple methods of producing professional types of candles.

It is a relatively simple matter to make a candle that looks good. Making a candle that fits a particular need—that burns well or gives a maximum quantity of light—can be an added challenge to the candlemaker.

Cooking up a batch of candles will provide hours of no-calorie cooking. Your candles can be every bit the ego trip of a beautiful cake or pie, and in addition they can match the decor of every room in your home. They also last longer than a cake, which gives more people a chance to admire them.

If you have never made a candle you may worry about special skills. It takes skill to make a cup of instant coffee. First, you must be able to boil water and not let the kettle boil dry. Second, you must be able to pour the water over the coffee without scalding yourself.

If you start candle-making with your "instant coffee" skills in good working order, you'll be well on your way to making beautiful candles.

Age may worry you. How old should you be? I've taught candle-decorating classes to "old threes." An "old three" is a child who no longer puts *everything* in his mouth.

I've also seen extremely senior citizens turn their newly acquired skills into extra income.

To pour a candle a person needs enough arm length and strength to control a wax vat. Short arms mean smaller candles and so most children can begin (with an ever-ready available adult) to pour their own candles when they are about ten years old.

Candles are a good family project. They cost little, require only minimum equipment, and give quick, "adult-acceptable" results. Children are usually so impressed by their success that they behave very well.

Older people enjoy making candles. Although physical strength may appear to be a problem, it really isn't. To pour most candles you can use ladles, basters, or pitchers if you need to. Very few candles require lifting more than three or four pounds of wax at a time. If you have only minimum strength to work with, accept the challenge of planning your project in such a way that it does not require great muscle.

Early History

Moses (in the Book of Exodus) created the first recorded candlestick. This candlestick held seven lamps, which were small containers of fuel with a wick inserted—not the candle as we know it today. The Bible states that Moses' candlestick was several feet high and would burn the night through on two wine glasses of pure olive oil per lamp.

According to Webster, candles are cylindrical pieces of tallow or wax with a wick running through them used to produce light. Mr. Webster might be shocked if he could see some of our modern candles, but then again, he might not. American Indians in Noah Webster's day filled dried fish with blubber and inserted grass wicks. I'm not sure which I would have found most objectionable, the smell of the burning blubber, the heat of the fish in my hand, or the speed needed to replace that grass wick!

Along the Pacific Coast there's a fish called the candlefish (a member of the smelt family, that is used for candlelight. These burn a wick of cypress bark.

The cylindrical piece of tallow or wax plus wick that Mr. Webster speaks of didn't come into use until late in the seventeenth century. This type of candle produced better light and was much superior to the old blubber and suet lamps.

In colonial America candles became a status symbol. The quantity and quality of light were the direct result of the productivity of the master and the creativity of his dame.

About 1855 Robert Bunsen studied the candle flame until he could make practical use of a burner invented by Peter Doedga and Michael Faraday. The Bunsen burner is still a popular source of heat and is used in a wide variety of places, from research labs to campsites. The principles that Bunsen discovered are the same as those used in the modern gas stove and in many modern heating devices. Robert Bunsen also seems to have been the first person who ever thought of a candle as a source of heat.

Next to moonlight, there is no more romantic light than candlelight. Modern, scientific, efficient man hasn't outgrown his desire for the romantic, nor has he advanced so far that he never needs candles for emergency use.

Today's candles have two components that we can depend on: a wick, and a grease or wax fuel for the wick. Closely related are many novelties made of wax that are referred to as candles but that are, in reality, wax craft.

We offer you standard formulas here. Try them. There are, of course, many possible variations of these formulas if you wish to obtain a particular effect. The more proficient you become the more likely you will be to demand that your special candle accomplish specific results. At that time you can alter the formula to suit your need.

Keep a notebook. Write down each experiment. Make notes of exactly what you are doing as you are in the process of doing it. Be extremely careful to keep the notes of your mistakes so you don't waste time and raw materials repeating them. (See figure 1, page 4.)

Don't forget to allow aging time for your candles. A wick should be aged at least two or three days after it is treated and before it is encased in wax. The entire candle needs another five or six days to age. Additional time should be allowed if the candle is very thick in diameter.

Age your candles where the air circulation is good. When the minimum time has elapsed the candle can be stored indefinitely.

Many candlemakers age their candles before they decorate them. This is especially practical when the decorations are three-dimensional, but it is also useful in all but the "soft" wax techniques.

4 | The Candlemaker's Primer

When the time comes for you to dress up your house for a party or contribute to the local bazaar or bring a special somebody a surprise gift, you'll have nothing to worry about. Your candle storage shelf will provide the answer.

Figure 1. A page from the author's notebook.

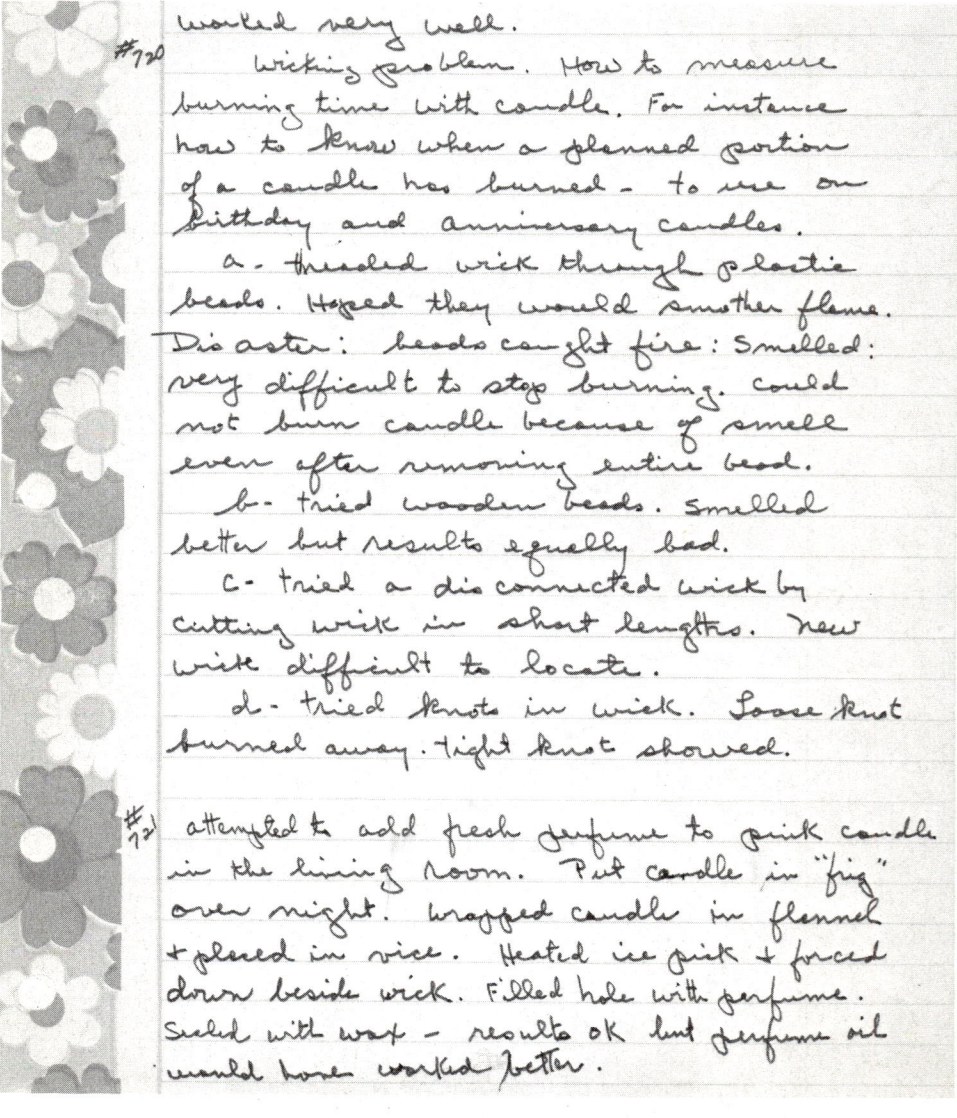

2

Waxes and Their Formulas

Waxes are of animal, vegetable, or mineral origin. They have varying resistance to heat and are unaffected by moisture or oxygen.

In candle-making, wax is the basic substance from which the body of the candle is created. The proper formulation of wax is second only to the wick in determining the ultimate success of the candle.

A word of precaution is in order. WAX IS INFLAMMABLE. It is just as inflammable as a pan full of sugar or cooking oil. Respect this fact. Never leave a vat of wax on an active heating unit. If the phone rings, or you must suddenly tend to a child, turn off the heat and lift the vat off the burner. The wax that is already fluid will hold enough heat to soften the wax that is still solid. Use the same precautions when working with wax that you use when you work with large amounts of grease or sugar.

If you should spill hot wax on yourself while candle-making, *don't try to remove it!* Saturate the area—wax and all—with cold water. You will do far less damage to yourself if you carefully peel the wax off *after* it has cooled than if you attempt to remove it immediately. Wax is airproof. Unformulated wax forms its own sterile bandage.

Selecting Waxes

There are no known waxes that haven't been tried in candles. The following information describes only the more popular waxes.

The recipes for candle waxes given here have been formulated around the most popular available waxes. If other waxes are available, try them carefully. Introduce them into a favorite formula in small quantities; be sure to measure. Check them carefully for their ability to take heat, to mix harmoniously with other ingredients, and for their contribution to the candle.

Waxes will vary considerably in the quantity of heat they require in order to become fluid. Use a candy or wax thermometer to learn the exact heat of any wax you are working with.

Keep in mind that the harder the wax the hotter and brighter your candle is likely to be.

Patio candles are an excellent example of why you need to vary your wax formulas. Some patio candles may be used as a source of heat to keep the coffee hot. Some provide light for a late evening meal.

Other candles can be very useful when spaced along the fringes of the lawn. These, usually formulated with citronella or an insecticide, will discourage insects. A cool-burning candle, with a high paraffin content, will chase bugs for quite some time. It is not usually necessary to burn these candles for the entire evening.

Still another set of candles might be placed near the garden walks or the terrace steps. Here, for the sake of safety, you need the very brightest candle you can make. To protect the border plants from too much heat these candles frequently are made with more than one wick.

In selecting waxes, consider the type of candle you wish to produce, the purpose of the candle, the candle's melting point, and last, but not least, the cost of the proposed waxes as well as the labor involved.

Base Waxes

Paraffin: In 1831 a method was discovered for making paraffin from wood tar. James Young of Scotland in 1850 established the procedure that is used today to distill paraffin. Today's paraffin may still be distilled from wood tar, but is more likely to be a petroleum by-product. It is an excellent foundation material, but used alone it melts easily, doesn't hold its shape well, and may not accept color as you would like it to.

The melting point of paraffin may be as low as 120 degrees, but paraffin with a melting point between 133 and 135 degrees is also available. If you have a choice, take the wax with the higher melting temperature. Paraffin may be purchased a pound at a time from your grocer or in eleven-pound blocks from craft shops, candle shops, and, on occasion, petroleum dealers.

Preformulated waxes are available in craft supply centers, hobby shops, and all candle supply shops. If you purchase such a wax from a general craft supply center be sure to inquire if the wax, when it was formulated, was meant for candle-making. Some waxes are specially prepared for batik and other crafts. Question their ingredients before you attempt to use them for candle-making.

Beeswax and bayberry, though one is animal and the other vegetable in origin, are both popular waxes that can be handled in similar fashion.

Beeswax may have been the first wax used to make a candle. Cavemen may have learned about it when they attempted to burn out a hive to get honey. For thousands of years beeswax has been used as a ceremonial candle. The bee has served man well with this by-product.

Early beeswax candles predate dipping and molding. They were made by rolling balls of the soft wax, then inserting the wick. This method is still used by some religious orders. The entire candle burns, so it is necessary to support the candle by placing it in a small glass or bowl. This is the practical reason behind the custom of using glass containers for religious candles.

There has never been enough beeswax to keep man supplied, and many laws throughout the ages have restricted the use of beeswax. Frequently the use of beeswax candles was restricted to the church altar. As a result, today beeswax seems to have a religious significance.

Cerosin wax is sometimes available. It is a refined form of beeswax and has all the lovely properties of its original form. Cerosin has a melting point ranging from 145 to 158 degrees. It is quite brittle when cold and frequently is combined with other waxes, especially paraffin, to make it less brittle.

Bayberry, myrtleberry, and *candleberry* are all related vegetation. Each plant has a small berry with a wax skin. These berries are desired primarily for their delightful odor. Many people also enjoy the mild, green color of the bayberry.

Myrtle is considered a symbol of love in some circles. For this reason some people believe burning a myrtleberry candle is a definite stimulant to romance.

The numerous fables about bayberry candles are part of their delight. Two of the most popular are:

> Bayberry candles, burned to the socket
>   bring luck to the house, food to the stomack,
> and gold to the pocket.

> These bayberry candles, when burning has ended,
>   assure you, good people, of fortune and friends.
> Not only at Christmas, but all through the year
>   shall their light be symbolic of hope and good cheer.

Cetin, or *spermaceti,* is the wax derived from whale sperm. Spermaceti candles are the standard for the measure of artifical light. The term "candle power" is based on the amount of light given by a pure spermaceti candle (112–115 degrees) weighing $\frac{1}{8}$ pound and burning at the rate of 120 grains per hour. Actually, spermaceti has such a low melting point that even the best candles made of it burn much too quickly.

Sterin or *stearic acid* can be purchased from the druggist, candle supply shops, or hobby supply outlets. Its melting temperature fluctuates between 120 and 190 degrees. This is a pure form of animal wax and is very practical for the majority of candles. It combines well with other materials, holds its shape, and takes a true color. It also makes paraffin opaque, a condition most craftsmen prefer.

If you are a purist and want something for the Pilgrim play at Thanksgiving, I'd recommend beeswax or bayberries plus stearic acid. Stearic acid could even be used for the entire candle.

The Pilgrims did not usually mix their waxes. Whatever wax was available determined what was used. No one of these waxes will make any better candle than the blend of two or more waxes.

Tallow is the one wax I rule out. Our pioneer ancestors made most of their candles from tallow. Having tried it, I'm convinced that the only reason for its past popularity was that it was much more available than other waxes. Tallow candles smoke excessively while burning and smell like burning flesh the entire time. Stearic acid is a highly refined form of tallow.

Candelilla wax is of vegetable origin. It is a harder wax than beeswax and melts between 149 and 156 degrees. It is extremely popular in Mexico and the Southwest.

Carnauba wax is obtained from the Brazilian palm tree, *Copernicia cerifera*. It is an extremely hard wax with a melting range between 184 and 196 degrees. Because of its extremely high heat and yellowish green color, very little carnauba is used in modern candles, except in small quantities, to increase the heat or lengthen the burning time of some of the softer waxes.

Cerin wax is nearly always an imported wax. It is a petroleum by-product and is sold according to its melting temperature, which ranges from 130 to 170 degrees. It comes in an assortment of weights and may be labeled *purified ozocerites, mineral wax,* or *cerin*. The Near East supplies much of the wax but some is also produced in other locations, including the U.S.

Chinese wax is created by a blight on evergreen trees that is common in western China. The melting range varies from 149 to 176 degrees.

Japan wax is hard and tallow-like and surrounds the kernels or berries of the sumac tree, *Rhus succelanea*. This tree is normally located in China and western Japan. The wax is hard and brittle but the melting range is only 122 to 133 degrees. It makes a fine candle.

Montan wax is an extract from the brown coal of central Europe. The wax is hard and brittle, frequently bleached white, and the melting range is from 162 to 190 degrees.

Ouricury and *Licuri,* other Brazilian waxes, and *Lanolin* (these may smell a bit when burned, so test carefully) are all used in candles with good results.

Sealing wax is not a wax at all but a combination of shellac and turpentine plus color. It *cannot* be introduced into a wax formula because of the heat of the wax, but it can be used as a decorating agent on the outside of a candle.

In addition, numerous *synthetic* waxes are now available that can be incorporated into candle formulas with good results.

Take into consideration the use you expect of your candle when it is completed. Does it need to be bright and give light, or are you going to use it to keep a serving dish warm? Obviously the heat available in some of the less popular waxes would be a plus if you desired extra heat. That same high melting point would help the candle hold its shape on a hot summer day. The ultimate use of the candle will affect the formula. If the candle is decorative, the color should also be considered when preparing the wax.

Hand-dipped candles are preferred and command a higher price in the market place than molded candles. For this reason, many molded candles have their outer layers dipped on.

The heat of the wax in the vat controls the thickness of the layer of dipped wax. The hotter the wax the thinner the coat and the faster you must dip to prevent the base wax from melting off. Wax stays fluid through a several-degree drop in temperature. The cooler it becomes, the thicker the coat that the dipped candle is able to pick up and retain.

To locate the temperature range in your wax, heat a small vat of wax until it begins to smoke. Remove it from the heat immediately to insure it does not get any hotter from the accumulated heat in the burner. Use a candy or wax thermometer and take heat readings from three or four locations (top of wax, outer edge, deep in the bottom, etc.). Average these heats. This is as hot as you can have your batch of wax and still use it safely.

As the wax cools stir in the skin that forms. As soon as the wax becomes so cool that it no longer dissolves the skin, take the temperature of the wax again. The average of these temperature readings gives you the coolest temperature of this wax.

Testing the heat range is important not only for new and strange waxes but also to check the formulation of routine waxes when you have a specific project in mind.

A candle will begin to distort and lose shape about 15 to 20 degrees below its fluid temperature, so the melting point of the candle wax formula should always be at least 10 degrees above the highest room temperature the candle will be exposed to. For example, a candle to be used during the summer where heat reaches 110 degrees should be designed to withstand heat of 120 to 130 degrees.

Formulas can vary considerably and are all correct provided the candle meets the need for which it was created. Paraffin can make up from 20 to 80 percent of any candle formula. Stearic acid usually comprises between 20 and 35 percent of the formula. Bayberry or beeswax can be used alone for the complete candle, but more often these waxes are mixed until they make up from 20 to 60 percent of the finished candle.

Candle Construction

Candles are put together in a number of ways. Most are dipped, poured, layered, or sculptured. Each technique produces a uniquely different candle.

No technique is simpler or more difficult than the others. As a beginner you should select the technique that best suits the kind of candle you wish to create.

Dipping was the favored technique of our colonial forefathers. They would stand by the vat with several wicks attached to a dipping rack (explained in Chapter 4, about equipment) and lower the rack to the surface of the vat repeatedly, until the wicks accumulated the desired quantity of wax. This was frequently a job done outdoors; the candlemakers would spend many autumn days making enough candles to light their homes during the dark winter days to come.

When candle molds were invented, they made the job of producing lights far less time-consuming. Pouring a mold not only is faster but guarantees the candlemaker a product identical to the inside of the mold with every single pouring. Poured candles have two liabilities that must be considered: First, the cooling wax contracts, which leaves a fissure (known as the shrinkage well) in the middle of the candle. This must be filled or it will interfere with the burning properties of the candle. Second, the poured candle is of one-thickness construction. The wick consumes the wax in a different way from a dipped or layered candle, and the poured candle will not burn quite as brightly.

Layering candles is a pouring technique explained in greater detail in Chapter 8. A mold is used, but the wax is poured quite differently. This different pouring technique creates a brighter-burning candle and eliminates shrinkage as well.

Dipped candles are preferred because they have bits of oxygen trapped between the layers of wax. This oxygen, released slowly as the candle burns, allows the wick to produce more light. Ordinary poured candles are a mass of wax. Any oxygen trapped in the shrinkage well is of no use to the wick, which thus has only the oxygen trapped within its own construction to depend upon.

When you layer a candle you also trap oxygen evenly throughout the candle, but the layers are much thicker and therefore fewer than in the dipped candle. There is no shrinkage well, so the candle is completed in one work session. Layering is faster than dipping but slower than pouring—until you remember that in straight pouring you must return to fill that well.

Sculpture techniques can be used to make an entire candle or in combination with other techniques. Frequently a good-quality commercial taper is used as a wick and core for a massive sculptured candle. Other candles can be enhanced by surface sculpture with techniques ranging from shallow relief to bas relief or deeper.

I prefer making candles in layers. This method simulates the better burning qualities of dipped candles by introducing more oxygen into the burning candle. Layering is also applicable for use with several different wax formulas, depending on what effect you desire.

Formulas

By far the most popular American candle waxes are paraffin, stearic acid, bayberry, and beeswax. Each makes its own contribution to the candle.

My favorite base formulas are quite simple. I have used them many times in the past twenty or more years and they have always been a success for the core or heart of the candle. If the candle core is "right," it is almost impossible to make a bad candle.

1. 67% paraffin
   33% stearic acid

2. 60% paraffin
   35% stearic acid
   5% bayberry or beeswax

3. 55% paraffin
   20% stearic acid
   25% bayberry or beeswax

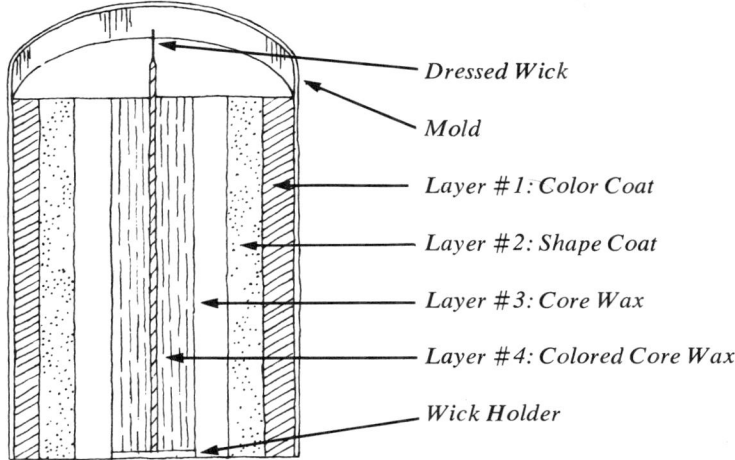

Figure 2. The construction of a "layered" candle. Pour the mold full of wax and empty it when layer has formed. When layer becomes both dull and opaque, pour the next layer.

When you make a bayberry or beeswax candle, you can use this formula: 25% paraffin, 35% stearic acid, and 40% bayberry or beeswax for the wick dip and again for dipping the final candle. This allows the candle to look, smell, and burn like bayberry or beeswax, but it gives a firmer base for longer burning and greater economy.

The quantity of wax to prepare will be important on occasion. Keep in mind that all the wax to be used together should be mixed at one time. This may not seem urgent until you are making more than one candle. Mix all the wax for a matched set of candles at one time to make sure that all will burn alike when you are using them.

To give you some idea of how much wax you need, keep in mind that 2½ pounds of wax usually melts to about 1 quart of fluid wax. This may vary slightly with some of the more unusual waxes, but it gives you a general idea of the quantities involved.

Dipping

Candles to be dipped are a bit different, since each dip removes some of the wax from the vat and the wax in the vat can get too shallow for you to finish the candle. A safe way to figure is this: If your candle is to be approximately 1½ inches in diameter, have enough wax when you begin so that the wax in the vat is about 3 inches deeper than the desired length of the finished candle.

Increase or decrease the depth if your candle is going to be an unusual size. For instance: if you are making a very fat candle or a candle longer than ten inches you will need to add more wax to the vat. If your candle is to be under six inches long and of a normal diameter you will need less.

If you ever get caught trying to finish a candle that is too long for a full dip in the wax remaining in your vat, you can turn your candle upside down or use your baster to help you. Submerge the candle as deeply as you can and then use your baster to put the wax around the top of the candles. Ladles have also been used in this capacity, but they don't get as close to the wick and

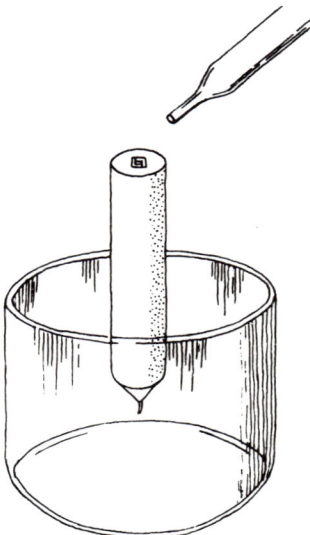

Figure 3. If you lack enough colored wax to dip the entire candle, turn it upside down and squirt wax on with your baster.

you are more likely to pour wax on your fingers holding the bottom of the candle.

If by this time the vat of wax has become quite cool, fill your baster with wax from the bottom of the vat. If, on the other hand, the vat is still very hot, fill your baster before you start to dip your candle. If the candle remains in a hot vat too long the already accumulated wax will start to melt off.

If you run short with more than two or three layers left to be dipped, you are better off adding more wax to the vat and starting in again when the new and the old wax are well mixed.

Shape

The candle must hold its shape. Many times, especially if the candle will be subjected to non-air-conditioned summer weather, it will be important to give exotically shaped candles a shell that protects the shape. Candles contained in bowls are safe, but any slender candle that stands upright can be distorted by heat.

I've always placed this protective shell between the decorations and color coat and the core of the candle. This allows the shell to function in two directions. Not only does it protect the entire candle from misshaping, but it protects the decorations (and the color) from melting while the candle burns.

For this shape coat I like to use 33 percent paraffin and 67 percent stearic acid or replace 10 percent of the stearic acid with one of the very hard waxes that has a high heat tolerance.

Color Coat

The color coat of the candle usually consists of a paraffin plus stearic acid formula with color added. The base formulas work very well.

For some effects you can even use pure paraffin plus color. This will not create an opaque color nor is it always a smooth, solid color so the addition of some stearic acid is valid. If you work with paraffin alone be sure to select a paraffin with the highest possible melting temperature.

Your completed candle needs to age. Five days to a week are not too long. Your candle will burn much better when it has completely aged.

If these are candles made for decor, there is no reason why they cannot age in the candlestick, on display. Only the burning of the candle requires aging, and if the wick has been independently aged you will be safe from sputters and splatters if someone else lights the candle before it is completely aged.

If you must burn a candle before it has aged properly, try freezing it for several hours alternately with thawing it completely. Three or four chill-thaw cycles in the refrigerator will age the waxes.

Problems

Always test everything in small quantities. Even if a new wax blends it may not improve the candle. If you test in small quantities you can use special waxes to their best advantage.

The simple truth about problems is that there is usually something you can do to rescue the wax if it goes wrong, even though you may not be able to make the candles you want at that moment.

One major problem of candle-making is underestimating the quantity of needed wax and running out before you have completed the project. This is a challenge discussed later in the book. Simply running out of the needed materials is a different problem.

If you were totally efficient you could plan ahead, but totally efficient people aren't necessarily creative and therefore efficient candlemakers are few and far between. Frequently you start with more than enough raw materials for the planned candles, then get a "brilliant" idea for making entirely different candles.

To meet these emergencies there are a few things you can do:

1. Keep an accurate inventory of raw materials with notes to tell you exactly where they are stored.

2. Keep all wax to be reclaimed ready for immediate use by removing the color coat before storage and marking unusual formulas on the candle core. (For example: You decide the green candle in the bedroom should be made over. Remove the green color coat and put it aside. Then you remember you added perfume to the core wax when the candle was made. Write the name of the perfume on a slip of paper and attach it to the candle before you put it with other candles to be melted down. You may no longer be able to smell the perfume but it may add a bit of scent to a new unscented candle, and it could conflict with the scent in another scented candle.)

3. Keep some inexpensive commercial candles in the studio to use as emergency wicks. They're totally surrounded with properly formulated core wax, and any candle wax surrounding this core will burn fairly well.

If you run short on a specialty wax such as bayberry, use the wax you have only for the final dip and put a few drops of bayberry scent in your core wax.

"Dirty wax"—meaning wax with an unappealing color—can be used for the bottom portion of the core of many candles.

All in all there are very few candle problems you can't think your way out of.

3

Cleaning and Reclaiming Waxes

Candle supply shops, hobby shops, and petroleum supply dealers will be able to supply you with clean, well-processed, pure animal or vegetable waxes. It is a rare day when these can't be purchased completely formulated and all ready to use. Sometimes you can save money by accepting a block of wax that has become dirty on the outside. It is a simple process to clean such wax for your own use.

ANIMAL WAXES: In the case of beeswax or any similar animal wax that is either shopworn or, as with beeswax, still mixed with honey, you proceed as follows:

Set a large kettle on a trivet in a larger pot of water.

If the raw wax is extremely dirty or the heating element is extremely hot, or if it heats very quickly, put some water in the kettle before you begin. Be sure the water is cool.

Break the wax into small chunks and add them to the kettle. There must be room for the hot water or air to circulate from the melting wax to the top of the kettle. If you have a very large kettle and a great deal of wax, put only part of the wax in at first and keep adding chunks of wax after the first wax begins to melt.

Bring the wax in the kettle very slowly to the melting point but DO NOT LEAVE THE ROOM while the kettle is heating. Stirring the wax occa-

Cleaning and Reclaiming Waxes | 19

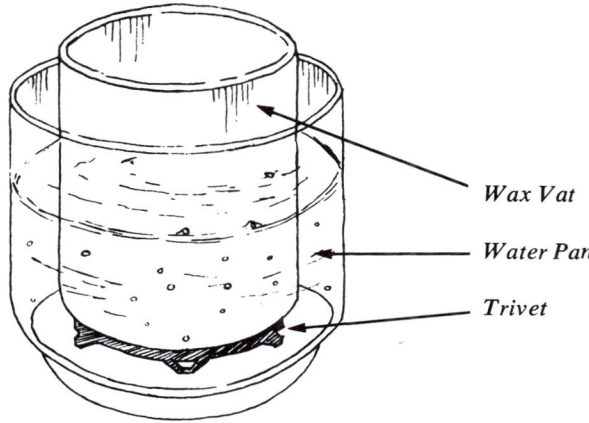

Figure 4. Always melt wax over water.

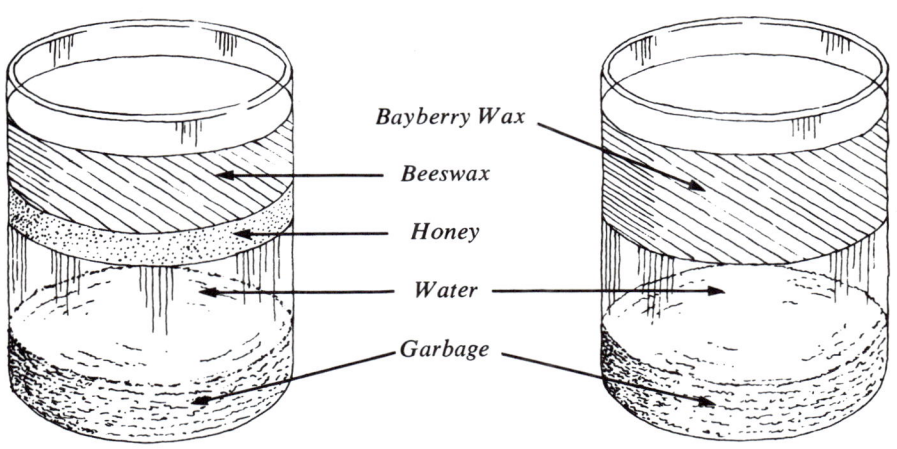

Figure 5. Cleaning either beeswax or bayberry wax follows the same procedure.

sionally will hurry the process. Measure the heat at the melting point with your candy or wax thermometer for future reference.

Cool the wax at room temperature. When the kettle of wax has cooled you should have a layer of pure wax on top of the kettle. Once in a while if the bee has been on an unusual diet you will have honey on top of the kettle, but this is very rare. There may be a layer of clean pure honey just under the wax. If you have used water in the kettle it will be beneath the honey. On the very bottom of the kettle will be a layer of all the dust, dirt, and impurities (see figure 5).

Strain the water in the bottom area even though the wax seems completely separated from it. This is most important if you plan to pour the water down the drain. A strainer lined with a nylon stocking or several layers of cheesecloth will catch all the small particles of wax that might otherwise clog the drain.

TALLOW: Suet, the extra accumulated fat on a mammal, is the source of tallow. It can be refined at home, if you don't mind the odor. Beef suet is considered to make the very best tallow but any and all suet from any animal can be used. It will not matter if you use suet from only one type of animal or combine the suet from several types of animals (such as beef, lamb, and pork suet). Proceed as follows:

Cut several pounds of suet in small chunks and place the chunks in a heavy kettle or skillet. Heat slowly until all the fat has melted.

The tallow should be poured off while still fluid and strained through several layers of cheesecloth. Many craftsmen like to reheat and re-strain their tallow two or three times.

VEGETABLE WAXES: Bayberry, myrtleberry, or candleberry come from related vegetation. Preparing the wild berries is as simple a task as cleaning beeswax.

Place the berries in the kettle, being sure to cover them with water. Bring the cold water slowly to a boil. Stir frequently but gently. Use a potato masher to push the raw berries under the water. The quality of your finished candle will depend on the pore structure of the wax, so be sure to start with cold water, heat very slowly, and stir gently for the best candles.

When the berries are cooked to a pulp take a temperature reading and record it for future reference.

When the entire mass is the consistency of fluid mush set the kettle aside to cool at room temperature. The completely cooled kettle will have definite layers of wax, water, and garbage in descending order.

If you wish to make a solid vegetable-wax candle, you should recook the wax in fresh water to further refine it.

If you break up the bottom layer of garbage and remelt it, usually additional wax can be reclaimed.

USED WAXES: Reclaim wax as a practical solution to experiments that don't quite live up to expectation or novelty candles you have tired of. You will be surprised at the amount of wax that can be reclaimed from the stubs of partially burned candles. This is not a difficult job. Keep track of the formulas used on your candles so you can use your reclaimed waxes to their best advantage.

To reclaim used wax, peel off the color and shape coats. This is usually easily done with a potato peeler. On occasion, if the shape coat is quite thin, it will be peeled off along with the core or color wax. This won't matter. In fact, it won't change anything except to make the new color coat a bit more brittle. Place all the wax of each color in a plastic bag until you are ready to reuse it.

Drop the core wax to be reclaimed into a kettle to melt. Don't worry about the wick. If it isn't easy to remove let the wax melt away from it; you can reclaim it from the bottom of the vat.

Be sure to label each batch of reclaimed wax. You will need to know what is in the wax when you wish to use it again. While the wax is still warm break it into chunks so that it will be easy to add to the vat when you reuse it.

Keep commercial waxes separate. Remember that a commercial candle is already formulated. When these bits and pieces (from different manufacturers and probably different formulas) are melted down they need no further formulation. In this day when all manner of different chemicals are being used, it is wiser not to mix commercial reclaimed waxes with hobby candle wax. But you may certainly add pure paraffin to commercial wax to increase the volume of wax available for your projects.

Be sure to label all your colors too, to indicate whether they are commercial or handcrafted. Try to include the ingredients used in the color coat waxes. This will give you better color control when you reuse the wax.

There is seldom a mixture of ingredients in a color coat, but you should know what the source of a color is. Commercial colors are ordinarily quite simple and color wax is not highly formulated. You can mix colored wax from commercial candles and from your own creations without any problems provided you remember the ingredients in your own specially mixed color.

When reclaiming any wax, remember that the dirt goes to the bottom of the vat. Remove the wicks first. Then, if you are in real need of every bit of the wax, strain what's left in the bottom through nylon or cheesecloth to purify it.

Color distorted by dirt will not be clear and bright, so avoid reclaiming the bottom of the vat when colored wax is involved. Usually the best place to use old, dirty wax is over the fuel used in your barbeque or fireplace. It will help the fire burn brightly.

Colored wax that has been peeled off can be stored indefinitely. Under most circumstances it will not need to be melted and refined but can be kept as is and added to another vat when the need arises.

If you do prefer to melt the color wax down, use a clean vat (tin cans are

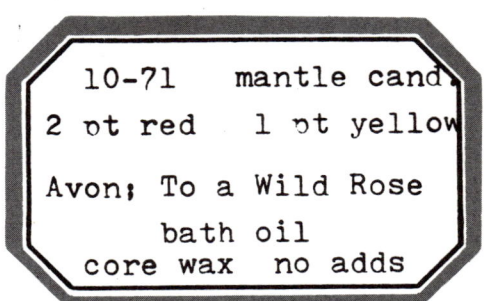

Figure 6. Label your colored leftovers. You may wish to remember the original candle. You need to know what the original wax and colors were. If you have added a fragrance it may appear to have faded with air exposure, but it could still conflict with a new fragrance when the candle burns. Last but not least you need to remember anything added to the wax that was unusual.

fine for small quantities). Heat slowly to avoid burning the color. The wax can then be stored in the tin can with a proper label and a tight cover (place the entire can in a plastic bag if you haven't a lid). You can also use muffin or cupcake tins to hold small batches of color. This will free your vat and may save you some storage space.

To pour "cupcakes" put a paper liner in each cup and pour the liners full of the colored wax. Let them set until firm, then label the contents of the wax and put them away until needed.

Keep each color and each fragrance separate. When you are ready to complete a new candle you may wish to mix colors or fragrances, but the purer the mix the better your chances of getting a nice, clear, fresh-looking and fresh-smelling candle.

A word of warning about reheating vats of wax. Wax expands considerably when heated, but it is different from the rising of a loaf of bread. When bread expands in the oven, it simply grows upward and the finished loaf of bread contains air holes. Bread is a soft substance. It does stretch and it will give.

This is not true of wax. Wax has to have room to expand, or it will explode.

Wax melts first on the bottom of a pot. By the time 1½ inches at the bottom have melted the wax needs "growing" space. If there is unmelted wax in an even layer stuck to the top of the vat, you have a problem.

Turn off the heat. Try to break up that mass of wax on top. Use a heated knife to loosen the mass of wax from the sides of the vat.

If you don't succeed in breaking up the mass or in cutting the wax from the sides of the vat, try the following:

Turn off the heat. Remove the wax vat from the pan of water. Bring the water to a boil and turn it off. Place the wax vat back in the hot water for 5 minutes.

After 5 minutes increase the depth of the water as much as you can and turn the heat on for 5 minutes. Turn off the heat and wait another 5 minutes.

In this manner—repeating as often as necessary—build the heat on the outside of the vat until the wax next to the sides of the vat has melted enough to allow the wax free movement. Then leave the heat on very low as the center of the wax heats.

24 | The Candlemaker's Primer

Storing Wax

Wax must always be stored as carefully as possible. Try to keep it clean. If you need to store a vat filled with wax more than two inches deep, let the wax cool in the vat until it becomes opaque. Take a clean can or even a drinking glass and push it down into the wax so that you lift cylinders of wax each time you remove the can or glass. This will allow for the needed expansion space when the wax is next melted.

The cylinders of wax can be stored on top of the wax remaining in the vat.

Lift cylinders of wax from the cooling vat to make reheating more successful. (Photo by Joe De Caro)

4

Equipment and Molds

Candle-making equipment can be as simple or as complex as you desire. If you wish to make only a few candles now and then, you should have as little cash investment and as much throw-away equipment as possible.

If you are planning to make candles as a real enterprise with an eventual cash return, it is then practical for you to set up a location where your supplies and equipment can remain ever ready for use.

Workshop

You need space and a cooking area to prepare the wax formulas; space to pour candles; space for decorating; plus space to store the aging candles, raw materials, and equipment.

Safety in your work area is important. If you begin with safety planning you will be more relaxed as you work. Photographers have red lights outside their dark room doors to indicate that they cannot be interrupted when the light is on. Such a device can also help the candlemaker to show other members of the household (or studio) that the wax is heating (and cannot be left) or that candles are being poured.

Asbestos should be liberally used in the cooking area. If you work in the cellar, and many of us do, the ceiling over the vats may be less than four feet above the cooking area. Heat rises and dries the ceiling. Cover this area of your ceiling with asbestos board. Use asbestos to cover your pouring table and anywhere else you might wish to put a vat of hot wax. The floor should be covered with many layers of old newspapers or something textured so that spilled wax cannot become slippery underfoot.

Small Equipment and Vats

Empty tin cans in any shape or size are always needed. Simply remove the paper label, wash, and dry. Then smooth the inner edge of the can opening—you may need to use a pair of pliers or a hammer to make sure there are no sharp edges left on which to cut yourself. Bend the rim of the can into a pouring spout. This not only protects you but also keeps the wax flowing freely. Any irregularities along the top edge of the can may keep the fluid wax from pouring properly, or if the can is used as a mold, may distort the shape of the candle.

You will need some smooth pebbles, several of one size and also a variety of sizes. These are used in the water pan to raise the vat, allow heat to circulate, and prevent trapped air or water from tipping the vat, as heat makes the trapped air or water expand.

Metal washers, small pieces of hardware material, or wick tabs from your candle supply shop—all in various sizes—are used to weight the base of the wick. It is important that these be clean.

A 1-cup ladle will help you in the formulation of waxes. However, any large soup ladle is a great aid in moving fluid wax from one vat to another. Ladles in other sizes are also useful.

A bulb baster of the type used in roasting is a good aid in getting wax into specific locations.

Cookie sheets with a raised rim on all four sides can be used as a mold for sheet wax and also under molds when you are pouring. The rim prevents the fluid wax from escaping.

Ice cubes should be handy, to use for testing and to stop leaks in paper molds. Hollow-centered ice cubes are excellent for color tests. You can make hollow cubes by emptying your ice-cube tray when the ice is half-formed.

Cupcake pans and paper cupcake liners are needed for testing and storing

Equipment and Molds | 27

small amounts of wax. They can also be used as molds for squat or floating candles.

Electric hot plates and warming trays—or any source of low heat—will keep the wax fluid while you work.

Heavy gloves, hot pads, old towels, and so on, are needed for lifting and pouring the vats of hot wax.

Small, simple wax vats can be made by placing a small tin can inside a larger tin can. The outer can is used for water and should contain either a trivet or pebbles on the bottom to elevate the inner can and allow for heat circulation. Larger but equally simple vats are made by using an old skillet with the larger size tin cans.

Home canning equipment is ideal for the very largest vats. So also is an old laundry tub, the kind once used to boil clothes in, provided it isn't so deep it's uncomfortable to work with.

Be on guard against any equipment made of plastic unless you know specifically that the plastic can withstand 300 degrees of heat. Galvanized pails once were used for melting, but a local fire chief has told me that modern solder can melt at 90 degrees. This means the bottom could fall from the pail before the wax is fully melted.

Other things can be used as wax vats. Coffee pots or well-balanced double boilers are excellent. But they will have to be cleaned if you are to use them for food again. A simple method of cleaning is to fill the pot as full as possible with cold water. Place it over a low heat and bring the water slowly to just below boiling point. Turn off the heat. The wax should rise and harden on the surface of the water. This process can be repeated until all wax disappears if you wish to be very safe.

Coffee pots and other equipment with pouring spouts should never be used with anything but clean wax. You must not clog your pouring spout. When you are ready to clean such equipment, pour hot water through the spout until the spout is free of wax, then clean the rest of the pot.

Ice picks are wonderful for starting wick holes, but if a pick is not available a length of wire can be used.

A wick wire from one to two feet long and from ¼ inch to ¾ inch in diameter is helpful. Some craftsmen keep a variety of these in different lengths and diameters. Put a wooden spool or paper tube on one end of the wick wire to protect your hands and notch or bend the other end so it can force the wick down into the candle but come out empty.

In addition, you should have:

Scissors for wick trimming.

A good fine-meshed strainer or tropical fish net for all discarded water to insure against pouring wax down the drain. Several layers of worn stockings, nylon net, fish filter, or cheesecloth have also been used successfully.

A notebook and pen for writing down all variations in formulation of candle wax or color wax.

Labels and cellophane tape for marking all unused wax. It is wise to sandwich your paper label between two layers of cellophane tape so the wax and dust cannot smudge the words away.

A timer to time the setting of a coat of wax. Time studies should be a part of your work program so you can judge and plan your candle projects successfully.

A thermometer to measure the temperature of the wax at its hottest and coldest points of fluidity. If a wax thermometer is not available a candy thermometer makes a good substitute.

Dipping Equipment

Wax vats 4 or 5 inches deeper than the longest candle you wish to dip.

Wicking of the same type used for other candles.

A small sharp knife.

A candlestick. Most candlesticks accept a candle of a standard ¾-inch width, but antique and handcrafted candlesticks have a wide variety of socket sizes, so it is important to custom fit candles for these.

Dipping rack or wick dip. Commercial racks are now available. You can also make your own by crossing two strips of wood approximately 1½ inches wide and ¼ inch thick. The length depends on the width of the vat and the number of wicks you wish to dip at once. Allow about 2 inches between candles. Make a handle from a coat hanger, a piece of doweling, an empty thread spool or any used drawer pull. Screws (to wrap the wick around once) and notches in the sides of the crossed sticks will hold the wicks in position while you dip.

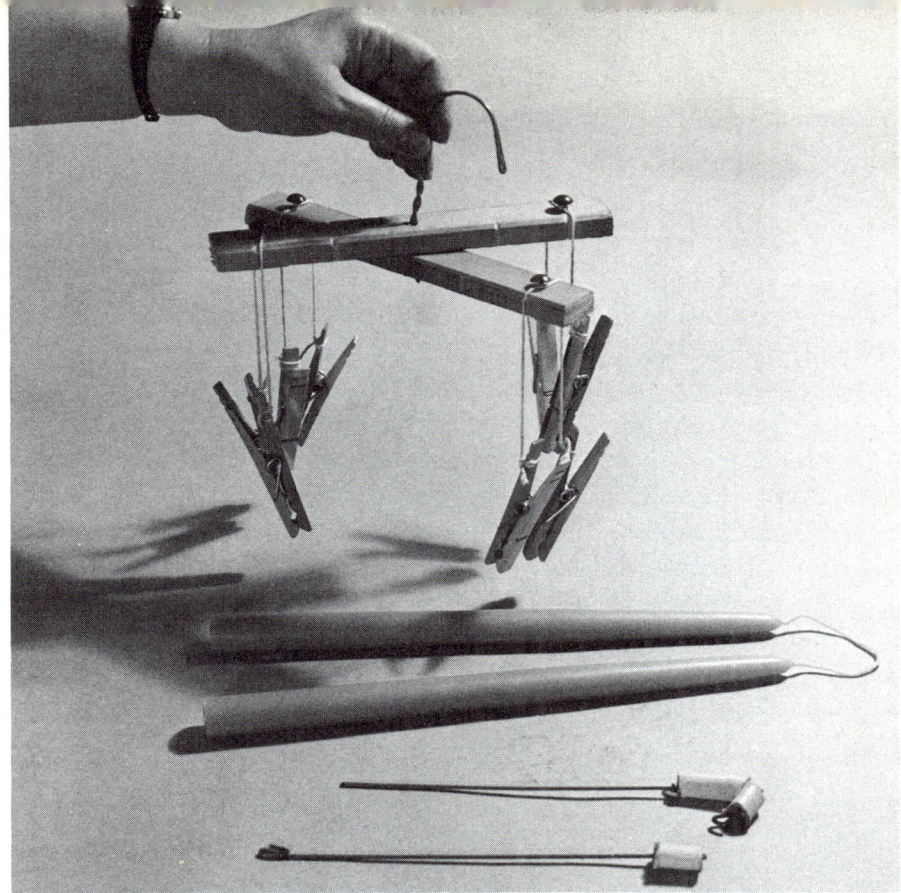

Equipment for dressing wicks or dipping candles is simple and you can, if you like, make your own.

The photo shows a dipping rack made from the top of a coat hanger and two pieces of scrap lumber. The hook from the hanger helps you hang the dressed wicks or dipped candles while the wax becomes firm.

Commercial racks that operate mechanically seldom have screws or nailheads to support the wick because they move up and down only. Manually operated racks, however, can tip while you are dipping or moving them about. The candle or wick might then slide off to the rack, but if your wick or wick holder is wrapped securely around the screw or nailhead, it cannot slide off.

The pair of candles shown still have their wicks attached, which is one method of producing a matched pair of tapers.

The wick wires are of two different styles because they do two different jobs. The upper wire, when heated, pokes the original hole into the candle. The lower wire, which can also be heated, has a hook at the bottom to which the end of the wick is attached. The wick is then forced down into the candle, and the wire is withdrawn. A knot in the wick end helps.

(Photo by Joe De Caro)

30 | The Candlemaker's Primer

Decorating Equipment

An egg beater, wire whisk, or fork. These all produce wax snow or froth.

A grater for wax coconut.

A grinder for wax granules.

Old kitchen silver. A knife for spot melting when you "sprig" decorations. A long-handled spoon for measuring small amounts of wax; bend the bowl horizontal to the handle of the spoon. Spoons of all sizes for various decorating techniques. Forks for texture. Mixing spoons to stir with.

A potato peeler for shaving color into the wax. It can also be used for shaving in decorating techniques.

Tweezers to place decorations on the candle and to pull the wick into a desired location.

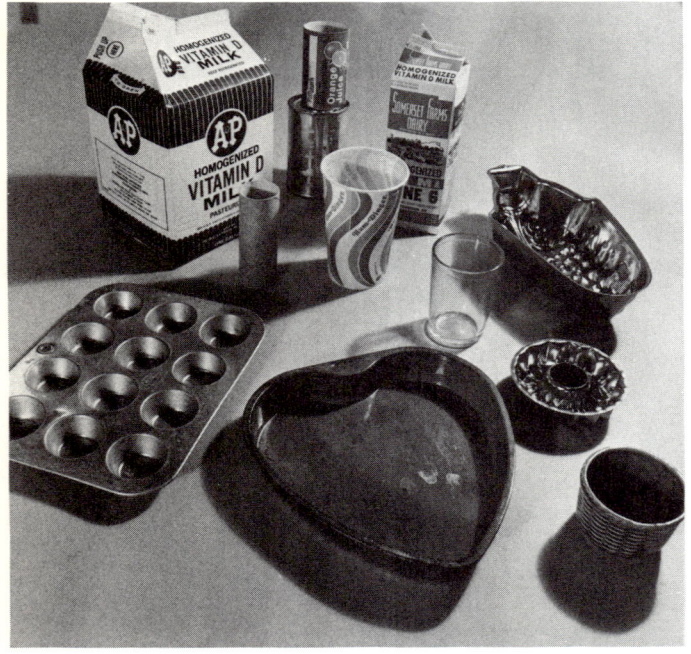

Molds may be anything
you can find in your surroundings.
Old dishes, gelatin molds,
and baking pans are all good but
equally useful are empty tin cans,
cardboard rollers from towels
or other such items and waxed
paper containers.
(Photo by Joe De Caro)

Molds

Molds may be of any suitable form. It is possible to buy both modern and antique molds from craft supply shops or antique shops. Modern molds come in a profusion of shapes and sizes and the majority produce a good, well-balanced candle. They also increase the expense of producing a candle and present a storage problem for the occasional candlemaker.

A search through your house will produce many, many things that can be used either as a mold or as a permanent shell for your candle.

Glass, metal, plaster, paper, and other materials may be used. Dishwasher-safe plastic can generally be used. Avoid undercuts, ridges, or anything that doesn't offer a smooth, obvious exit for the candle unless you intend to have it remain in the mold permanently.

Candles that do remain in the mold can be fascinating. This is a way to use up the odd dish or glass or miscellaneous bric-a-brac.

Paper containers such as milk, cream, and cottage cheese cartons work very well as molds. Paper tubes make long, slim display candles.

Other good molds are clean, empty eggshells, hollow plastic fruits or vegetables, or children's "squeaky" toys.

Those big shells the kids insisted on carting home from the beach are great to light the garden path and filled with a citronella wax will also chase their weight in bugs.

Clean, empty tin cans in almost any size or shape make good molds. An old rubber ball, split open on the seam line, can be used for round candles.

Molds commonly used for salads or desserts make lovely candles. Molds in fancy shapes—now rare—that were once used for butter can also be used. Old candy molds also make fine candles.

Bowls of various sizes can serve as molds for the tops of mushroom-shaped candles.

You'll find other things around the house that will come in handy for candle equipment. Be careful or the garbage man will be leaving your house empty-handed!

| 5 |

Wicks

The candlewick has presented a challenge to man since prehistoric times. The materials used have evolved from grass or rush to twigs, skins, cloth, thread, and finally string.

The invention of the "flat" wick was a great step forward. With the coming of cotton and linen thread man learned to twist a wick. The twisted wick burned more steadily, and gave better light with less smell. When man learned to braid, he had a way of producing a wick that didn't ravel in burning. Queen Victoria used the new braided wicks for her wedding and thus greatly speeded their acceptance by the world at large.

Earlier, Benjamin Franklin wanted more light for his desk. He wasn't pleased with having light from several candles because they took up too much space. Experimenting, he tried many variations. However, it wasn't until he placed two wicks in the same candle that he found a way to increase the quantity of light.

The value of borax or boric acid in wicks was discovered about the time of the Revolutionary War. Until that time the ash from the wick had been a continuous problem, causing smoking, and drowning the flame with its weight. The borax or boric acid made the wick self-consuming and vitually eliminated the smoke problem.

This seems like a very small thing in view of what man has been able to create in lighting equipment since then. Actually, these were the foundations upon which all modern lighting was built.

The good candle burns with a bright flame, gives off no offensive odor, does not drip, and needs no snuffing. The proof of the candle is definitely in the burning, which is controlled by the wick.

Wick Materials

Hobby shops and candle supply shops sell wicking very reasonably. It is excellent for most candles. It comes in a dozen different sizes and is usually processed to burn well. You can also use a reasonably priced commercial candle as a wick.

When you have progressed to the point that you design candles with special performance features in mind, you may want to make your own wick.

Any soft string, linen, or cotton yarn may be used. The larger the diameter of the candle, the heavier the wick should be. Linen requires more heat to burn than cotton, and it is what you should use if you want your candle to give maximum heat. Bleached yarn (with the resulting pore change) will burn more evenly than unbleached fibers.

Size of Wicks

A wick needs to be approximately 3 inches longer than the candle it goes into. If you are producing one wick for a specific candle this length of wick is sufficient.

Most of the time you will produce wick to be used at a later time with no specific candle in mind. Three lengths of string, each five to six yards long, will make several candlewicks and can be a comfortable length to braid.

Preparation of Wicks

1. Take one length of string and dye it with food color or dot it every few inches. You can use any coloring agent available that does not affect the burning properties of the string.

2. Braid the colored string with two lengths of plain string. The tighter the braid the cooler the flame.

3. As you braid, pull the colored string very straight. When finished braid-

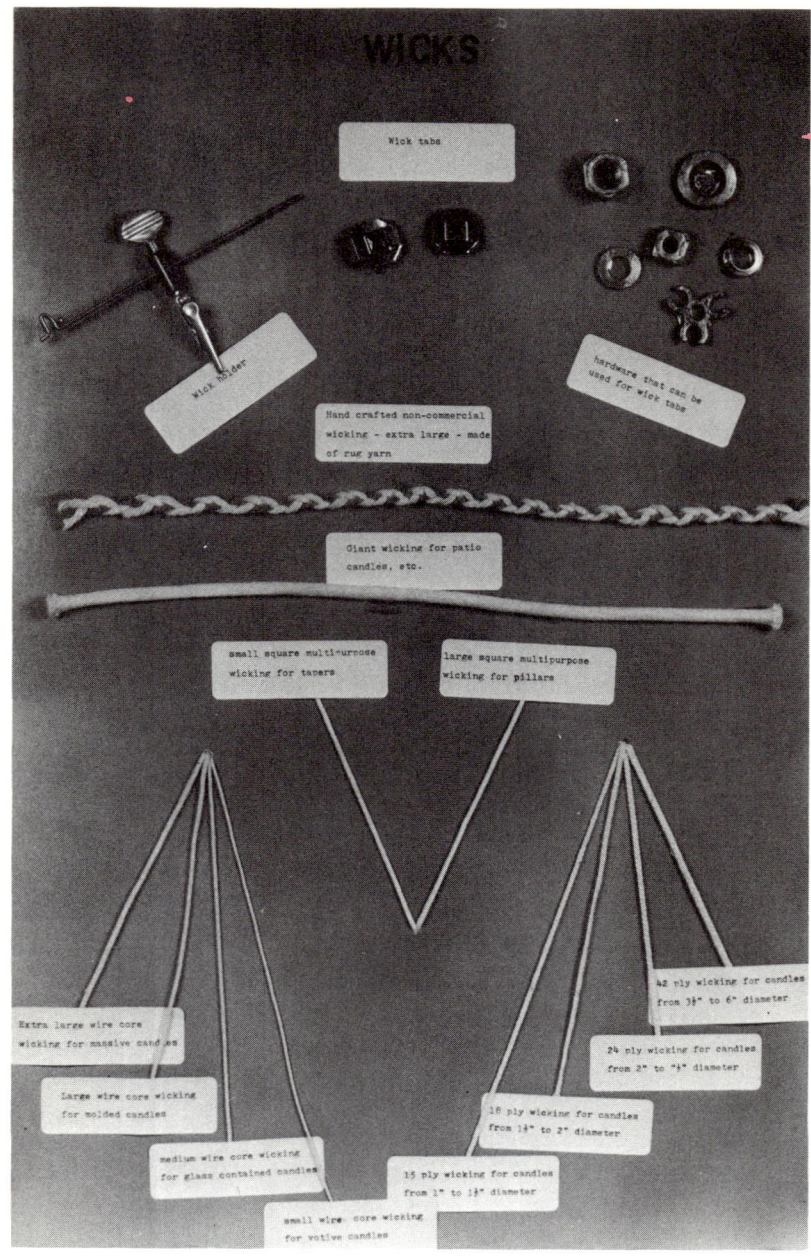

Wicking and wick equipment come in a vast assortment of sizes, so you can tailor the wick to the candle. (Photo by Normandy)

ing, work the other two strings until the colored string is completely straight. This makes your candlewick burn better, as the straight string will carry the flame while the other two lengths will protect the oxygen supply.

4. Fasten both ends so the braid can't unravel.
5. In a container with a tight cover mix the following:

   2 tablespoons table salt
   4 tablespoons borax
   2 cups warm water

Shake the container until the solution has dissolved.

6. Place the braided wick in the solution to soak. You can soak several braids of wick together with no problem. Just be sure you have more fluid than dry wick. The wicks should be well saturated and then left to soak at least two hours.

7. Dry the wicking completely by hanging it where the air circulates. I loop my treated wicking over a clothesline or a towel rack. After three days (when it is cured) I roll it into a ball and put it in a drawer.

8. When you are ready to produce a candle, cut a length of wick 3 inches longer than you intend the finished candle to be. Fasten one end of the wick to a washer or wick tab. Fasten the other end to the dipping rack or a clip clothespin and dress the wick.

9. To dress the wick, dip it in fluid wax (use a good basic core wax) and then hang it to dry absolutely straight. Repeat the process until the wick is at least ½-inch thick with wax. Your wick must be kept absolutely straight and rigid from then on.

Flame

The candlemaker should understand something about candle flame. A burning candle creates a treadmill type of action. Candle flame is a combination of hydrocarbon and oxygen. The units of hydrogen and oxygen unite to create the heat, which burns the carbon. Carbon burns with a yellow glow. (Other chemicals, which produce flames of other colors, are discussed in the following chapter on color.)

The burning wick sucks up the melted wax or fuel to create heat, which then melts more wax which the wick then sucks up, and so forth. Light is the happy by-product.

Determine in advance the ultimate use of your candle. If the candle is to produce heat, your construction should emphasize introducing as much hydrogen and oxygen as the wick can produce. If the candle is to produce light, the quantity of light will be affected by the quantity of carbon.

Since the vast majority of modern candles are needed only for minimum heat and for soft light, the hobbyist can keep to the middle of this road and have excellent results.

If the quantity of burning and melting are not synchronized the candle will be unbalanced and will not burn properly. If the flame and the amount of melted wax are not in harmony—a phenomenon referred to as guttering—the resulting drip will run down the side of the candle, an unwelcome nuisance. Guttering may be the result of imperfections in the wax formula, but first check the following wick problems. It is far easier to change a wick than to remake the entire candle.

Wick Problems

Before you change the wick check the following:

1. Is the wick pointing a bit off center? The burning tip of a good wick points to approximately the angle of 3 minutes past noon or 3 minutes before noon. Don't try to insert a wick at this angle. You need to worry about the angle of your wick only if the candle doesn't burn quite right. At that time put the candle out. Remove any ash from the wick and take out any fluid wax that has accumulated. Tilt just the tip of the wick and then relight your candle. If your burning wick is not functioning well and already seems to be bent a bit, try turning the candle around so the air currents in the room approach the wick (and candle flame) from a different angle.

2. Is the wick too small? This makes the flame slow to consume the amount of melted wax available.

3. Is the wick too large? It will burn too hot for the quantity of melted wax and therefore consume wax too quickly. The candle then burns unevenly. The flame will begin burning nicely, then flicker as it almost runs out of fuel. When a new fuel supply has melted the wick will again burn brightly for a moment, only to flicker and sputter again.

1. Wick should point a bit off center.
2. Is wick too small?
3. Is wick too large?
4. White ash, too much Borax
5. Black ash, too little Borax

Figure 7. Wick problems.

4. Is there too little or too much boric acid or borax treatment of the wick? If this is so, the wick will burn unevenly and leave an ash, which may smoke or appear rigid. Too little borax (or boric acid) will produce a black ash, which may smoke and contain unburned fibers. Too much borax (or boric acid) is likely to show a white ash, which is rigid in appearance. The rigid ash may cause the melted wax to run down the outside of the candle.

To change the wick for any of these conditions run a hot wire down the side of the offending wick and gently pull the wick out. Enlarge the hole until you can insert a new wick that is more suitable.

6

Color and Design

Flame Colors

Candles can be colorful in a variety of ways. Much depends on where and how the candle is to be used and burned. Few people seem to realize that the flame on a candle can be colored. If you like fire-gazing try grouping a few candles with colored flames in your fireplace. The resulting effect on a summer's night will provide all the dreaming with none of the heat. The colored flame can be equally exciting in a floating candle.

To color the flame of a candle you must change the wick solution. If you have a jar of wick solution already mixed, you may add additional chemical salts. You may also mix fresh wick solution substituting the chemical salts for the table salt.

Chemical salts are available in small quantities wherever supplies for children's chemical sets are sold. Larger quantities come from chemical supply houses. Be sure to buy salts, since these are water soluble and will combine best with the wick formula and the wax formula. Some other forms of the chemicals may work, but under *no* circumstances use nitrates, as these are explosive.

You can have an interesting range of color by working with barium, which burns green (from chartreuse to grassy), copper for the blue green shades, and strontium for the reds (sometimes a blue red but more often orange red).

Color and Design | 39

These colors are never exactly predictable, since there are great variations in the strength of the chemicals and in the chemical content of the tap water.

If you are mixing fresh wick solution try any of the following formulas:

1. 2 tablespoons salts of copper
   4 tablespoons borax
   2 cups warm water

2. 2 tablespoons salts of barium
   4 tablespoons borax
   2 cups warm water

3. 2 tablespoons salts of strontium
   4 tablespoons borax (or boric acid)
   2 cups warm water

4. 1 tablespoon table salt
   1 tablespoon chemical salt*
   2 tablespoons borax
   1 cup warm water

5. 1 tablespoon table salt
   1 tablespoon salts of copper
   1 tablespoon salts of barium
   1 tablespoon salts of strontium
   8 tablespoons borax or boric acid
   3½ cups warm water (You may have to increase the quantity of water to dissolve all the dry ingredients.)

You can also try other combinations of the chemicals. If your wicks aren't uniform in burning or don't change color enough discuss the problem with your supplier. The strength of the chemicals can vary, as can the chemical contents of the water.

Soak your wick just as before. If you wish to use a commercial wicking you may. Treat the soaked wick just as you treat uncolored burning wicks.

One variation that gives startling results is created by soaking the strands of

---

* Meaning any one of the three chemical salts listed in nos. 1, 2, and 3, or try the salts of other chemicals.

the wick before you braid it. Soak each strand in a different color. Decide which color you wish to be dominant and make this the straight strand of wick, then braid just as before (after the strands have been soaked and dried).

Wax Colors

Pigments to color waxes must be wax- or oil-based. Since this type of pigment is abundant, this presents no problem. Purchasing colors can be as simple as buying a box of children's crayons at the local store, talking the local cosmetics buyer into parting with lipsticks of strange colors that haven't sold, or picking up a few tubes of oil paint at the local art supply store. If you have a hobby or candle-craft store nearby, you can buy color pats specially designed for candles.

I like children's crayons for both their economy and the efficiency with which they may be used. I purchase refill boxes from a school supply house, which gives me boxes of crayons all in one color. The crayons come in both normal size and extra-thick kindergarten size. The heavier crayon is useful for shaving, for deep-colored candles, and for some decorating techniques. Normal-sized crayons can do all these jobs but not always as quickly.

If crayons aren't available you can switch to oil paints. These can be purchased either at an art supply store or at the counter where oil-based house paints are sold.

Don't try to use house paint. Oil-based house paint has additives of other chemicals that are not designed to be beautiful when burning. Tubes of pigment used to color house paint follow much the same formula as artists' paints so they will mix well with hot wax, but house paint itself does not.

Considerable publicity has appeared about using fabric dye to color candles. I have seen some breathtaking results, but they are few and far between. There is a problem here, caused by the differences of heat value. If the fluid heat of the wax and the maturity temperature of the dye coordinate, all is well, but if the dye requires more heat than the wax you can wind up with no color at all. If on the other hand the wax requires more heat than the dye, it will probably cook the color out. In other words, color tends to disintegrate if more heat is applied than required. This sometimes shows in a change of hue. Other times overheating will result in no color at all or a smudgy gray or sluggish brown.

The problems with dyes that require only a little heat can be lessened by cooling the wax to its lowest point of fluidity. Add twice the color you think you want and stir hard (but not so vigorously as to introduce air bubbles). Pour the wax just as soon as you get a smooth color.

If the dye requires more heat the answer is patience. Heat the wax until it is fluid. Add the dye and stir, and stir, and stir. Eventually the dye will dissolve despite the lower heat of the wax. Since you are working at the top heat of the wax be very careful not to push the wax into a fire-hazard condition.

Color-Testing and Formulas

The best way is to test the dye and the wax in small quantities before you use the larger vat.

Colors alter in hue with changes in temperature. Some of the most beautiful pastels look like dirty white when the wax is still hot. This is of no importance to the finished candle but it is all-important to understand when preparing the wax. The only way to know that you have a color, or the right amount of color, is to keep testing your batch of wax.

Color-testing a batch of wax is not difficult. Put a few drops of wax on white paper. If you are working hard to match a color or seeking a particular shade, drop your wax on a piece of glass (you can use the outside of a wide drinking glass or a Pyrex pie plate). Looking through the glass toward a good light, you will be able to see the exact shade of the color in the vat. If you are matching colors, using glass will enable you to see both shades side by side.

There is more to color-testing than just seeing the color. You should also be able to determine whether the color is evenly mixed throughout the vat. The best test for this is to pile up a few drops of wax from several different parts of the vat. One-ounce glasses can be used to hold the wax samples. Even better are hollow ice cubes.

Fill a normal-sized ice-cube tray with water and place it in the freezer. When the cubes are a little more than half-frozen empty the fluid water and you'll find a hollow cube. Pile the wax, a few drops at a time, into the hollow and when the wax solidifies cut it in slices. If you are not positive the color is even, look at it through a magnifying glass. Your color chip should always be at least ¼-inch thick to enable you to judge the color. A thickness of ½ inch or more is safer in determining if the wax is evenly colored. Under normal circumstances any color variations will show in streaks, giving the wax a layered look.

To remove wax from the vat for color-testing, I use a metal iced-tea spoon with the bowl bent horizontal. This allows me to get wax from several locations and several depths in the vat, a few drops at a time.

When you check your vat to see that the color is evenly mixed make one more test. A casual glance at the filled ice cubes will tell you whether the layers of wax are adhering to one another or curling at the edges. If the layers peel apart (and this seldom happens), you have some foreign element in the mixture that could be part of anything new you've used. Try adding more paraffin. This alters the color very little, but paraffin is so congenial that it frequently cures the problem.

If the batch remains rigid and brittle, don't throw it away. Set it aside, well marked, to use at a later date. It will sponge for interesting texture, create three-dimensional decorations, or make floating candles.

Guard against muddy colors. Be sure you don't make a dirty-looking candle. Most colors that seem muddy will clean up with addition of white. If you are aiming for a dark color, try adding black. Some blacks will help to clear up a muddy color, others won't.

If you are thoughtful enough to keep track of how you color your candle you can prevent dirty, muddy shades. Remember that the three primary colors (yellow, red, and blue) when mixed together in equal quantity will become various shades of beige, brown, or gray. Add black or white and you lighten or darken the hue. Let one primary color dominate and you have a muted color. Let a secondary color—green, orange, or purple—dominate, or let the combination of primary colors become unbalanced, and the color looks dirty and muddy.

Neither black nor white can usually do much to improve a basically dirty color. Experiment with a small amount of the wax, especially if you like muted shades, but if the color does not clean up quickly and easily, it is better to make a new batch.

Mark the ingredients of the off-color wax. There are places to use the wax where its color won't be seen.

Artists seldom mix primary colors when they want good, rich-looking browns and grays. They prefer to mix red and black for brown, or pale blue

Color and Design | 43

and black for gray. These combinations, toned with white, are faster and more dependable to work with.

There are many muted colors on today's market. But I have found that I frequently get better results when I blend two colors of wax for the effect I want.

In one experiment I wanted a dark, murky, dull-green candle. After some unsuccessful attempts at getting the right hue, I used the following procedure: The entire candle was dipped in fluid wax that had cooled as much as possible. This wax was in the shade of green I had in mind and I gave the candle two dips, waiting between times for the first dip to become completely dull.

When the color coat was firm but still warm I used a baster and dripped hot gunmetal-colored wax over the candle. I held the candle by the wick over the vat and allowed the excess gunmetal-colored wax to run off immediately. The result was not a solid color, since running wax varies in thickness, but the variation in shades is so gradual you aren't aware of it unless you are actually handling the candle. This way I got the color I wanted.

Mixing your own colors is an adventure in itself. Much depends on how original you want to be. Some colored candles are easy to buy while others are never available, even in the better candle stores.

Mix experimental colors in small quantities. I usually work with 1 cup of fluid candle wax and grate my crayon into a ⅛-teaspoon measure. By keeping track of proportions I get an idea of how much I want of each color. For instance: 2 parts medium green to 1 part white, or 2 parts lemon yellow to 1 part kelly green.

When the color is as I want it, I use the same proportions in the big vat. The proportion of wax to color is a lesser problem since the final color can be softer or bolder but the hue will remain the same as long as I keep the same color proportions.

If you enjoy a challenge there is no limit to the possibilities you can create when you mix candle colors. To start off, here are some combinations; you can add your own variations.

Use standard, popular-brand crayons and mix:

    1 part bright red, 2 parts black to obtain a lovely rich brown
    1 brown, 4 gold for burnt orange
    1 brown, 2 orange for bittersweet

1 true blue, 1 true green for deep jade
1 white, 1 medium blue for ice blue
1 red, 2 green for moss green
1 red, 4 white for pale cream color

Planning new colors will be easy when you develop mixing skill, but until then work with these quantities (they may vary a bit due to manufacturing changes):

1 normal crayon will color 1 quart fluid wax to a warm shade
1 inch from a tube of oil paint will color 1 quart fluid wax
3 inches oil paint will tint 1 quart fluid wax a lovely clear color
6 inches oil paint will tint 1 quart fluid wax an intense color
1 color pat (available at candle shops) should tint 20 pounds of solid wax

Fabric dyes differ in intensity by brand, by water reaction, and by manufacturing procedures. Read the label on the box carefully. Usually a 1-ounce package of dry dye will color 50 percent more wax than 8 ounces of liquid dye. Check the recommended heat of the water. You will have the most success using these dyes if you can match the wax heat to the water heat. This probably means purchasing a package of dye requiring water from 150 to 180 degrees of heat. Measure the wax (I usually put 1 cup of wax in a separate vat until I work out the color) with an accurate measuring device. Use your measuring spoons to add the dye. Stir the dye until it has blended with the wax and then color-test the result. Once you have the desired color use the same proportions to mix the larger vat of wax.

Oil paints and dyes need far more mixing and stirring than crayons. Candle color pats produce an even color with little effort, while crayons also give smooth color with little effort, provided the entire vat of wax is stirred after the color is added.

Be sure to color all the wax needed for one candle or for a number of matching candles. This is the only way to be absolutely sure the colors will be uniform.

When you run short of colored wax there are three remedies that can be used successfully:

1. If you are color-pouring in layers, push an empty tin can (or anything

If you ran short of colored wax
for your first layer you must act
quickly to prevent this
outer layer from blemishing.
Force anything available down into
the wax. Don't touch the outer
edge of wax but force the
object down into the fluid wax
until the wax level rises
to the top of your proposed candle.
(Photo by Joe De Caro)

else available) down into the center of the fluid wax until the outer layer is forced up to the very top of the proposed candle.

2. If you are pouring a solid color candle and have at least two-thirds of the needed wax, fill the top third with paraffin, core wax, or any uncolored wax available. The distance of the pouring pitcher from the vat will vary the effect. The color may blend over the entire candle or the candle may become two-colored. If you are using a glass mold you can see the results. Another effect is possible if you agitate the wax until the top color is variegated or smoothes out to a paler shade than the bottom. You can rarely get the entire candle the same lighter shade by this method.

3. Quickly tilt your mold and rotate it at an angle until you get a color coat all the way to the top of the mold. Pour off all the fluid wax. Add to it enough basic formulated wax to fill the mold, then pour the outer layer over again.

Don't stop pouring even two minutes and then return to continue pouring the outer layer of the candle. It is almost impossible to have a smooth surface if you once stop midway. The surface of the mold grabs the outer layer and cools it just enough to make an ugly ridge that penetrates the entire layer. (See photograph, page 56.)

It is far safer and surer to pour all the wax back in the vat, clean the mold, add enough wax to the vat to make up the shortage, then repour. The color may be slightly paler, but this won't be important unless you are matching the candle to something else. If you are matching, then method 3 is by far the most satisfactory. If the outer skin of the candle is the desired shade it won't matter if the inner candle is paler in hue.

Store leftover colored wax either in its color vat (cover it well to keep the wax clean) or by pouring cupcakes. Label your cupcakes carefully. You can see the color of the leftover cupcake but you need a label to tell you the ingredients of the wax base and the component parts of the color.

Your base ingredient should be indicated: paraffin? core wax? brand "D" candle wax? Jot down the formula for the wax. The color proportions are even more important and should be carefully indicated: 1 part yellow, 2 parts red, 1 part white, etc.

If you label thus you will avoid mixing orange red with a red that contains blue (orange and purple are not likely to give you a desirable color). Another reason for labeling is that you may not have enough left of a particular color wax when you next wish to use it. Since few people have totally accurate memories, you need the label giving color proportions to help you make more of the same color.

Try to make the color and design of your candle harmonious. If you become a professional candlemaker, you will want to study the interior decorating magazines and follow their trends.

There are some basic design principles to help you. Your design, to be pleasing, should have harmony and contrast.

Contrast can be provided either by a startling shape or by a different, eye-catching color. It can also come from different intensities of a selected color scheme.

Harmony of shape, pattern, and color is very important. You have not only the simple shapes such as squares, oblongs, and circles to choose from, but also complicated combinations of these shapes. Color and pattern can be provided by stripes, plaids, or geometrics. An elaboration of the basic teardrop shape becomes a daisy or paisley pattern. Squares plus distorted triangles become houndstooth. Generally speaking, any of the shapes from nature, such as flowers and leaves, combine well with one another.

In thinking of your finished candle design you should first consider where and how the candle is to be used. If the candle is to add to a mood of gracious relaxation try softened colors and a repetitive pattern. If the candle is to become a focus of interest try an intense color and a pattern contrasting with the surrounding decor.

Have the courage to try what interests you. Beauty is in the eye of the beholder. Remember that many artists and craftsmen have not been popular with their immediate peers. Josiah Wedgwood, for example, was thrown out of his family's potteries for producing the very vases we cherish today.

7

Fragrances

Fragrances, like colors, must be oil-based or of a waxy substance to blend successfully.

Choose your fragrance carefully, with the ultimate use of the candle in mind. Try your favorite perfume. Experimenting, to add a third dimension to your candle, is well worth the time and effort.

Some candles, such as bayberry, beeswax, and candles that are colored with lipstick, will have natural fragrances. These will probably need no further fragrance treatment.

Fragrances may be introduced into the custom-crafted candle in two ways:

1. Put drops of the desired fragrance on the dry wick before dipping it. Let the wick absorb the odor before it is given its wax dressing. Once the liquid has been absorbed into the wick you can treat it just as you treat unscented wicks.

2. Add the desired fragrance to the core wax so that it is burned as part of the fuel when the candle burns.

Many fragrances will immediately evaporate if added when the wax is hot. Wait until the first skin appears on the top of the wax vat. Add the desired quantity of fragrance, stir until the skin is dissolved, and the scent will be distributed throughout the wax. If the skin doesn't blend into the vat and melt readily, it can be lifted out and put aside to be used when you are again heating the vat.

Make a test candle if you are not sure of the scent. Pour some wax into a cupcake pan. Insert a wick or use half a birthday cake candle for a wick. Chill the wax. Smell the candle. Light the wick, allow it to burn until the candle wax has begun to melt, and then smell again.

If the fragrance is too shy, increase the quantity of perfume or whatever was used. If the fragrance is too strong, increase the wax content.

Wicks seldom contain too much aroma. Keep in mind that perfume evaporates in the air and the candle will lose some of its aroma while waiting to be lit. You are more likely to have too little than too much fragrance.

To increase the quantity of scent from a given candle you can easily add fragrance to both the wick and the wax.

In either method, the quantity of fragrance is a matter of personal taste and should be governed by the use for which the candle is intended. An antiseptic or disinfectant kind of candle will certainly require a more dominant odor than a candle for the buffet table.

Fragrances are stocked by any candle hobby shop, but your druggist can supply you with many oils that will give your candles a delightful and unique aroma. You might start by trying the following:

> oil of sandalwood, or any of the oriental incenses
> oil of spearmint, or patchouli, or others of the mint family
> vetiver, a tropical grass that adds an exotic touch
> oil of cloves, for a spicy scent
> pine, bayberry, and frankincense,* delightful for Christmas
> citronella, excellent for an outdoor summer candle. You can introduce various disinfectants and antiseptic properties by adding sulphur, eucalyptus oil, or iodine.

Check your scented candles carefully during the curing period. Once the moisture has disappeared, store them in airtight containers to preserve the fragrance.

* Olibanum is the modern name for frankincense. If your local druggist cannot supply it you might try the Kiehl Pharmacy, 109 Third Avenue, New York, N.Y.

8

Pouring Your Candles

There are two kinds of molds: home-created molds and commercially produced molds. There are many minor differences but the major difference to the candlemaker is that the commercial mold is poured from the bottom to the top, which guarantees a perfect top on the candle.

Candles from home-created molds need a bit more work to produce a perfect top. Generally speaking, they are poured down from the top. This leaves the craftsman the challenge of creating a nicely finished top. Each time you attempt a molded candle of a different shape you must consider how to pour so the finished top of the candle pleases you.

The following direction will assume you are using objects found around the house. Instructions (unless otherwise specified) will tell you how to pour from the top to the bottom.

1. Select a solid, level surface on which to pour your candles.
2. Cover the surface with thin asbestos paper. This can be purchased at most hardware stores. Next spread out several layers of newspaper.
3. Now line a four-sided cookie sheet with waxed paper or aluminum foil and place it on the newspapers.
4. Place a small bowl of ice cubes and a basin one-quarter filled with water nearby. A pitcher for extra water is also useful.
5. Pour your mold while it is sitting on the cookie sheet: This allows any

If hot wax opens a seam, or a paper mold begins to seep wax, you can quickly "heal" the leak by rubbing the area with an ice cube.
(Photo by Joe De Caro)

spilled wax to remain clean and within a confined area where it can be reclaimed and reused.

6. If your mold leaks, and this can sometimes happen with a break in the solder of a tin can or a seam opening in a paper container, the quick remedy is to stroke the leaking area with an ice cube on the outside of your mold. Once in a while a paper mold will form a bulge. You may like the looks of the bulge if the entire container bulges symmetrically but if the bulge is only in one area, the quick solution, again, is to rub the entire area with an ice cube.

Once your mold is poured it can be moved into the basin of water to quicken the cooling process.

A word of caution: If any wax spills on the floor be meticulous in cleaning it up, as spilled wax can be extremely slippery.

Be sure the inside of the mold is completely dry. Any water left inside a mold will mark the outside of the candle. These water spots won't matter on an opaque container if you are not going to remove the candle from the container. They will matter, however, on a transparent container or on a candle that is to be removed from the mold. Removing the blemish can be quite a problem. Dipping the candle usually leaves dimples.

Determine where the top of your candle is to be in relation to the top of a mold. This is important if you are not utilizing the entire length of a mold. Mark the top with pencil, pen, china marker, or tape on the inside of opaque molds. Pour just to this mark.

As I said earlier, I prefer to pour candles in layers. Hand-dipped candles are in far greater demand than molded candles because they burn better. The many layers of wax picked up in dipping trap minute particles of oxygen, which help the candle burn more evenly.

A. Pour first layer of the candle—the color coat.
B. Pour second layer—the shape coat.
C. Pour third layer—the core wax.
D. Place the wick.
E. Finally, fill remaining space with colored core wax. The complete candle has a smooth top and no shrinkage cavity. (Photo by Joe De Caro)

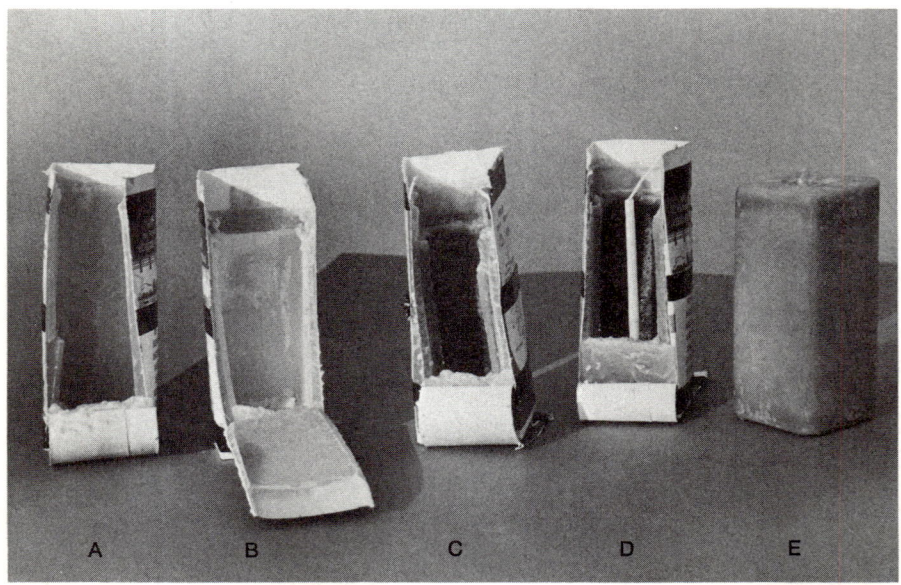

(Left) Commercial molds produce beautiful candles. An ever increasing assortment is available at candle supply shops. They do, however, increase the price of making a candle.

You could hardly run a professional studio without molds but in the beginning, when you are probably producing just one candle of each kind, consider whether you'll want a second candle from that particular mold before you buy it. Color photo by Fred Keesing.

(Below) Use bowls for mushroom caps. You can have as many differently shaped mushrooms as you have bowls. When the wax in the bowl is opaque force in a well dressed wick that is long enough to protrude into the mushroom stem. Next place the stem mold over the protruding wick and pour the stem full of wax.

If you use a length of paper tube, for a stem, cover the tube with wax and allow it to remain as part of the candle. Stems, such as the one pictured, can be poured by using a section of the neck of a plastic bottle. Color photo by Fred Keesing.

(Above) Try placing some gay plastic flowers inside your mold and pouring white wax over them. Color photo by Fred Keesing.

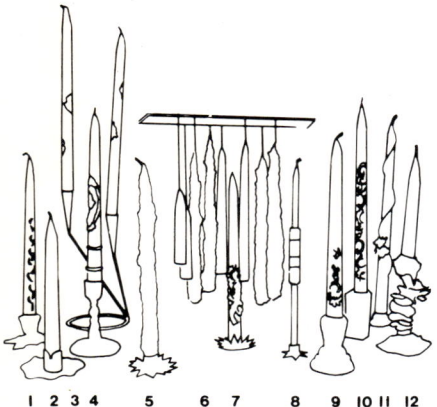

There is a tremendous variety of things that can be done to tapers. From left to right:
1. Black candle hand painted with red wax roses.
2. White taper given a topping of gold wax with a paint brush.
3. Tall candles in back were dipped in shiny wax and decals used to match the decor in a special room.
4. Gold candle is victorian in mood. Uses bright braid, decoupage, and very fine glitter.
5. This orange candle was treated with whipped wax, color dipped and then rubbed with a metallic paint to give gold tones.
6. An assortment of "curing" candles on the cooling rack. Some have been dipped in froth.
7. The red candle has an applique of grapes cast in wax.
8. You can also decorate with stripes of colored beeswax.
9. This white candle is hand painted and gilded.
10. Appliqués of paper foil.
11. A rolled beeswax candle with fluted edges.
12. A taper with hand made sweet peas.
    Color photo by Joe De Caro.

(Right) Twists can take several forms. Here is a twist that can be sculptured by pouring a long mass of wax and using basic sculpture tools. Color photo by Fred Keesing.

(Below) This is a large candle, almost three feet high, which had colors dipped and dripped and allowed to run. Photo by Fred Keesing.

(Above) You can buy beeswax in a honeycomb pattern in thin sheets. Here is a small hive made by carefully rolling the beeswax into a novelty candle. Color photo by Fred Keesing.

There are many sculpture techniques that can be used in candlemaking. Betty Thomforde likes working with a special sculpture wax to turn egg shaped candles into roses and put dainty ruffles on a tree. The mushroom candles can be shaped while the wax is still pliable. Photos top and right by Joe De Caro. Photos of tree and mushrooms by Fred Keesing.

Pouring Your Candles | 53

Layer-pouring means pouring from the outside to the inside of the candle, not from the bottom to the top or top to bottom. The universal problem of all poured candles has always been a center cavity that forms when the cooling wax shrinks to the outer edges of the mold. This fissure is of uneven size and frequently hides deep in the candle, making it difficult to fill. When you pour a candle in vertical layers you can eliminate the shrinkage-well problem.

The exterior of many candles you can purchase (especially in warm weather) has two distinct layers. The extreme outer layer, in this book, is referred to as the color coat. This layer is never very thick—sometimes less than ⅛ inch of wax—and its entire reason for existence is to provide the candle with color.

Immediately under the color coat there is frequently another layer of wax, which is opaque and very white. The wax appears to be quite different in pore structure from the wax elsewhere in the candle. The function of this layer, which contains additional stearic acid or high heat wax, is to help the candle hold its shape, no matter what the weather. This is what I call the shape coat.

Either of these coats of wax can form the layer next to the mold itself. You can also add these layers by dipping the candle after the inner candle has been completed in a mold.

The usual procedure for a molded candle is as follows:

1. Determine the top of the candle by marking the inside of the mold. Now pour the mold full of whatever wax you've chosen for the outside of the candle.

2. When this layer of wax has formed and is between ⅛- and ¼-inch thick, empty all the remaining fluid wax back into the original vat.

3. Allow the mold to sit until the shell of wax left in the mold appears dull. To hasten the cooling and prevent undue gravitation of wax to the bottom of the mold, you can stand the mold in a basin of water while the wax sets.

4. If necessary, remove the wax from the pouring area of the mold so that there is a clean line at the top of the candle shell.

5. Pour the next layer of wax reaching up to ¼ inch from the top of the first shell of wax you poured. If the first layer was the color coat, this layer will be the shape coat. (If the first layer was the shape coat, this layer will be

the core wax.) When this layer is ⅛- to ¼-inch thick and appears opaque, empty the remaining fluid wax once more into the vat.

6. Wait again until the wax is dull. Clean away from the pour spout the wax left when you emptied the mold.

7. Pour additional ¼- to ½-inch layers of core wax, following the procedure above. Keep all the layers level at the top with the second layer of wax until the hollow area in the middle is about 1 inch across. The number of layers will depend on the diameter of the candle.

8. When the hollow part of the candle is about 1 inch across (this will vary with the size of the candle and the size of the wick you are going to use), pour a puddle of wax in the bottom about 1 inch deep. When a skin forms on the puddle place your wick in position. Make sure the wick is straight and supported at the top of the mold.

9. When the puddle of wax has become completely opaque and the wick seems firmly in place, pour the rest of the candle. If the outer layer of the candle was completely formulated color wax, you may wish to pour this inner part of the candle with the same color wax. If it was color but not a formulated wax, fill the candle with core wax, stopping at the same level as the other inner layers of wax.

10. If this is a color candle (but the colored wax was not formulated) wait until the wax around the wick is opaque and then pour the unformulated colored wax on top of the inner layers of wax to give you a smooth, professional-looking top.

11. When the candle becomes firm enough to handle remove it from the mold. If a metal mold has been well greased or treated, the candle should slide out. Paper molds usually need to be torn away. A tin can mold may need to be placed in the refrigerator for a few moments. If this doesn't contract the outer wax of the candle sufficiently you can cut the bottom from the can and push the candle through. Glass and metal molds that don't easily release the candle can be treated in one of the following ways:

Increase the shrinkage by chilling the mold. This can be done by placing the encased candle outside on a cold day or in a pan of ice water or in your refrigerator.

Soften the outer wax layer by exposing the outside of the mold to heat or hot water. This soft wax will allow the candle to slide out of the mold.

Pouring Your Candles | 55

12. You can now dip the candle in another coat of wax if need be. A quick dip will cover up blemishes in the present color coat or give the candle color if you started pouring with the shape coat. When this other layer of wax is firm you may decorate the candle immediately or put it aside to age.

When you create a candle so large that a final color dip becomes impractical, you can use the following method of adding color:

In an empty vat set the candle on a brick or overturned bowl—anything that will raise the bottom of the candle above the bottom of the vat. This vat can be quite shallow. It should be wider than the candle and very clean. If you have a turntable (you can use a lazy susan), place the vat and the candle upon it.

Pour the color coat slowly and as evenly as possible over the candle. Rotate the turntable as you work. When the color wax has stopped running from the bottom of the candle, the candle can be gently removed from the vat. Slide an egg turner or a sharp spatula under the candle to release the wax. Set the

Stand giant candles in a vat
on a turntable. As the candle
rotates pour the candle color.
Be careful to pour
the color as evenly as possible.
(Photo by Joe De Caro)

56 | The Candlemaker's Primer

candle aside to age and use the wax that remains in the vat for another candle.

Pouring in vertical layers eliminates the shrinkage cavity. It doesn't matter how many layers are poured, nor is it vitally important that the layers be of any specific thickness unless the layering is important to the design of your candle.

Some craftsmen are more meticulous than others. If details are important to you there is no reason why you can't time the setting period for each layer of wax, especially if you are going to burn several candles of the same design together.

Running out of wax will not affect the candle's burning qualities and will not hurt the candle's appearance if it happens while the inner layers are being poured. The outer layer is different.

If you lack enough wax in the pouring pot for the outer layer, you will have to remedy the situation immediately or your candle will show patch lines. Remedies for this situation are covered in the chapter on color (see pages 45–47).

If you run out of wax you have
only a minute to refill your pitcher
and start pouring again.
This candle was left
too long. That odd white line is
where the original wax stopped.
This line is very difficult to
hide by decoration.
(Photo by Joe De Caro)

Glass Containers

Extreme care should be taken if you are using glass as a mold, especially antique glass. Glass and china are prone to internal shock that doesn't show on the outside but can crack open unexpectedly. Since good glass and most glazes contain lead, if you cut yourself, have the cuts examined by a doctor.

Treat glass containers gently. Work patiently and don't pour until after your wax has formed a skin so you know the wax is at the coolest possible pouring point. Warm the glass mold by standing it in a shallow container of warm water. Pour as slowly as possible but pour continuously.

Paper Molds

MILK CARTONS: Paper molds such as milk cartons are themselves put together with wax. As you pour hot wax into them, the container wax sometimes melts. This at the very least warps the candle and at most breaks open a seam in the container and allows all the hot wax to flow out.

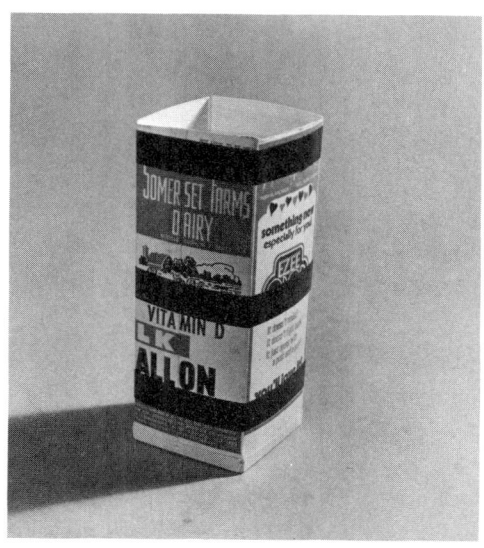

Bind your waxed paper molds with heat resistant tape to prevent seams from opening and to prevent the paper from bulging and warping. (Photo by Joe De Caro)

58 | The Candlemaker's Primer

To prevent this, try the following simple remedies, alone or in combination:

1. Work when the fluid wax is as cool as possible. Keep the container cold until you are ready to use it. I find this works especially well with very small molds or shell-type candles.

2. Bind the paper container with bands of adhesive tape, masking tape, or anything that will adhere to wax and is heat resistant.

Use three bands on a one-quart milk container (one at the top edge and the other two at about the ⅓- and ⅔-positions on the container). Reinforce large paper molds with the same bindings plus vertical bindings at the corners and seams.

3. If your paper container has a seam completely around the bottom edge you may prefer to stand it in water (in your basin) while you pour. These containers are very light. To keep them steady place a heavy metal washer or other weight in the bottom of the container before trying to pour in the hot wax.

When you remove your candle from the mold you can either leave the weights to make the candle more secure while it burns or you can remove the weights by one of two methods. You can saw off the bottom layer of the candle or you can dig out the weights. In either instance one or two dips in a vat of wax will have the candle looking very nice with no evidence of the weight removal.

4. Keep a bowl of ice cubes handy to rub the outside of the mold if it begins to bulge or leak. Pour cold water into the basin as soon as you have completely poured the outer layer of wax.

Paper molds leave a candle with a dull finish. This can be remedied by a quick dip in the color vat, or by polishing the candle with a soft cloth and a bit of cooking oil or grease.

TUBES: To use a paper tube or similar mold you must plug up the bottom. With adhesive tape, or any sturdy heat-resistant tape, fasten the bottom of the tube to a flat surface (saucer, sauce dish, pie plate, etc.). Pour a bit of hot wax around the outside of the tube with your baster. Pour one or more baster's-full of wax inside and wait for this to become dull and firm. If the paper tube is a large one you may wish to fill the dish outside the mold with

Stop up the bottom of a paper tube by binding it to a shallow dish. Next pour a puddle of wax around the outside of the tube and chill it.

The number of layers you pour depends on the diameter of the tube. A simple way to insert the wick is to suspend a well-dressed wick from a lead pencil just before you pour the final layer.
(Photo by Joe De Caro)

crushed ice. Thin paper tubes seep and must be bound with tape along their entire length.

You can pour paper tubes in layers but the number of layers is dependent on the size of the tube. Just before you pour the inner layer insert a weighted, well-dressed wick. I find that tying the wick around a lead pencil will hold it nicely in place until the candle is completed.

CONES: Paper soda-fountain cone-shaped cups give interesting effects when inverted. Try this procedure:

1. Place a bit of crushed ice or ice water in the bottom of a drinking glass.
2. Place a paper soda-fountain cone into the drinking glass for support.
3. Pour a thick layer of colored wax, making sure the paper cone sits absolutely straight at all times. If you'd like a textured effect try pouring with your baster. Circle the inside of the cone again and again with spurts of wax until the layer of wax has reached the desired density. For a very symmetrical candle use several of the cones together. The added strength will help keep the shape.

Done with brown wax, with the peak opened, this becomes an Indian tepee. Cut the peak off and open a "door" while the wax is still soft. If you leave this

To pour wax into a soda-fountain cup, which usually comes to a point on the bottom, first prop it in a drinking glass containing ice water. (Photo by Joe De Caro)

candle hollow you can put a votive candle inside which will cast a shadow from the door and cause smoke to issue from the top opening. A hot darning needle will pierce designs into the wax. A long wick on the votive candle will smoke more than a short wick.

Use a beige color wax, pour the cone hollow, place it on its side while still soft, use your fingers to shape it a bit—and you have a cornucopia. To increase the "basket" look use your baster to run drops of wax down and around the sides. Start by working with one drop of wax at a time. If the children are "helping" you, let them play with small amounts of extra wax to shape the fruits and vegetables. They can be painted at another time.

Another way to use cone-shaped candles, in any color, is to remove the peaks and carve the sides. They can then be used in place of candlesticks. Here is an ideal solution for odd-sized candles. If the candle is large and heavy, the cone of wax should be large and solid. If it is a small candle, you need a cone only an inch thick.

You can poke holes in any color cones (use a hot ice pick) and place greens or flowers in the wax.

A chimney candle with wax froth "snow." (Photo by Joe De Caro)

For a Christmas tree use deep green for the outer layer. With a sharp knife cut small holes or ornament shapes. Pour the second layer in another color.

CHIMNEY CANDLES: An always popular candle using a milk carton as a mold is the chimney candle. If a milk carton isn't available, the same candle can be made in other containers.

Use a pint carton, or cut a quart container to the desired height. Pour in a ½-inch layer of brick color (usually red). Pour next an equally thick layer of shape coat. This layer can be white or the same color as the brick.

When the wax is firm remove it from the mold. With a sharp point cut horizontal ridges around the candle about ¼ inch apart. Some craftsmen like to cut all the way through the color into a white under-layer.

Place vertical cuts at intervals to simulate bricks. Remember that bricks are staggered to give the wall strength so you should cut only from one horizontal line to the next, then from the middle of that brick cut down to the next horizontal line.

Thick white poster paint makes wonderful-looking mortar for these bricks, and a crust of white foam wax around the top gives the appearance of snow. Burn a votive candle inside.

If you remove the bottom from this candle, lighting it will be easier, but some people keep the bottom and use long-handled matches to light the votive candle.

Tin Can Molds

Tin cans make fine molds. They should be greased well with shortening, vaseline, or tincture of green soap before pouring. After the wax is firm you sometimes must destroy the mold to remove the candle, as the can's top and bottom seams and one vertical seam will usually trap the candle. Cut the bottom off the can and push the candle through. If you are making identical candles it is usually less trouble to use several identical cans than to try to reuse one can.

Pour your tin can mold just as you would pour any other candle mold. Some people do not find mold seams objectionable; certainly they are often seen on commercial candles. If you wish to eliminate the seam, pare off the mold mark so the surface is smooth. Work smoothly and evenly with a small sharp knife.

You then can polish the candle with cooking oil on a soft cloth or you can dip your candle in a coat of color or transparent wax. Paraffin is the easiest wax to use for a coat that is either transparent or translucent.

POURED TEXTURE: It is easier to pour texture in a tin can mold than to add the texture after the candle has been removed from the can. Some cans have ridges in the tin that run in a horizontal pattern. Such ridges hold the candle tight so it can't be unmolded. But this doesn't mean you can't use such a can. Wet the sides and pour out the water, leaving the inside of the can damp. Insert a layer of heavy burlap or a well-fitted strip of corrugated paper. If you are not sure these linings are heavy enough, you can place light cardboard between them and the wall of the can.

The damp sides should hold the lining in place. Pour your candle. When it

Tin cans usually make good molds if they are smooth. The candle in the can on the left is hopelessly trapped because the ridges in the can will not release the candle. Heating the can will only melt the candle and create a mess. Line cans like this with heavy corrugated paper or anything else that will keep the wax out of the can's ridges. (Photo by Joe De Caro)

64 | The Candlemaker's Primer

is firm remove the candle with the lining intact. Peel the lining from the candle and you should have a most interesting texture.

When you have become more advanced in candle-making, try glueing plastic leaves to a cardboard liner. When you peel away the liner you will have the leaves embossed into the wax. This is called intaglio design. You may have to clean the wax edges of the design. Another method is to pour one very thin layer. Remove the liner and open it at the seam just enough to cut away the wax from those plastic leaves. Reinsert the liner into the can and pour again in a different color.

Finish this candle as you would any other. When you remove it from the mold you'll have colored leaves on whatever background you have selected.

There are other textures you can pour. Fit two cans together, leaving a space of about an inch between the larger and smaller can. Place a weight inside the smaller can.

Sometimes when you pour a textured candle you get an air pocket at the bottom. In this picture, you can see the area that is not textured. A simple solution is to cut the candle shorter, but you can also add sea shells or some other decoration to hide the flaw. This candle is textured with vermiculite. (Photo by Joe De Caro)

Fill the area between the two cans with something to create a texture. Any of these will work:

ice cubes	aquarium gravel
coffee grounds	small clam or snail shells, etc.
vermiculite	rice or pasta

Since many of these items are quite light and will tend to float, it is wise to place a net over the top of your mold. Be sure your texture material is packed evenly all the way to the bottom of the outer can or milk carton. Cover the entire top of the mold. Usually a piece of nylon net, cheesecloth or even a fine hair net will hold the texture material in place. A rubber band or string wound around several times and tied will secure the net. Most nets will not interfere with pouring the wax between the cans but start very slowly and if you find the mesh of the net impedes the flow of the wax you may have to slash a hole in the net large enough to pour through.

Pour your wax in the space between the two cans. Sit the outer can in a pot of water and also fill the inner can with water. When the wax has solidified you should be able to pour the water from the inner can and remove the weight.

Now remove the inner can. If you use ice as a texture material be sure to drain out all the melted water. Use a paper towel or napkin to soak up any water clinging to the wax. Use a heavy shape coat to prevent the texture material from burning along with the candle and pour the core of the candle as you would any other.

When the candle is removed from the can the texture should be in full view. If there is a layer of wax on the outer surface it should be removed. A dip in very hot water is usually the easiest way to remove the excess wax. You can dip several times if the effect pleases you.

A few more words about ice might be said. Make sure to blot the water on the inside of the shell with paper towels or napkins before filling it with core wax, since any remaining water will sputter and steam when the hot wax is added. You can vary the size of the holes caused by the ice by making your pieces of ice larger or smaller. A variety of sizes of ice will create a swiss-cheese effect. Uniformly sized round ice "cubes," carefully placed, can make your candle look almost like a stone wall has been removed. The wax never melts the ice with total uniformity since the heat of the wax will vary as it pours past the ice. If the candle is poured in color you will have a glow almost like lace when it burns.

Kitchen Molds

The average kitchen has an exciting assortment of materials to make candles with. It would be difficult for me to say which item needed to be greased and which did not. If you normally grease the utensil for hot food it should also be greased for candle-making. If the mold is specially coated (for instance, with Teflon) and you need to work with a sharp instrument, it is wise to remove the candle from the mold before you cut, and then replace it in the mold.

Wax is a cooperative material. Techniques can be varied to suit the circumstances.

MULTICOLORED ORNATE CANDLES: Using an ornately designed mold for two or more colors of wax can be fun, but it does take careful craftsmanship.

Pour the entire mold with background color. Pour out the fluid wax while the skin of wax is still thin. With a small sharp blade, carefully remove all the wax from the important parts of the design you wish to make in another color. For instance, if the mold has a bunch of grapes, remove all the wax from the grapes. If you are going to use a third color, also remove all the wax from the leaves, for example.

To add the other colors you have two methods to choose from:

You can pour the entire mold in a second color coat—in the above example, this would be the grape color—and remove this second color from the leaves. Then you pour the entire mold in leaf color and proceed as you would for any other candle.

The second method works well if the design is not delicate or extremely scattered. With a spoon, a baster, or an eyedropper, place the grape-colored wax in the grape design. Place leaf-colored wax on the leaves by the same method. When this wax is firm pour another thin coat of the background wax and then proceed as you usually would for any candle.

If this candle is to be a symmetrical one, proceed with the method described above for symmetrical candles. Since people cannot look at both back

Gelatin molds can be used in a variety of ways. Cake and salad or dessert molds can produce strikingly different candles.
(Photo by Joe De Caro)

68 | The Candlemaker's Primer

and front at the same time, small variations of color in the design won't matter.

Squeaky-Toy Molds

Many children's molded plastic "squeaky" toys can be used for candles. Test them to make sure they don't melt at wax temperature. A small piece of the plastic covered with the hot wax should tell the story.

These can be poured just as you poured the gelatin mold, or you can use the following procedure:

(Left) Plastic toy bottles produce a milk bottle shaped candle. The original plastic was split all the way to the base, but it need only have been split as far as the mark on the second bottle since it releases very easily.

(Right) The plastic apple came from a fruit arrangement. It was cut open and then taped together. The patch of tape on the blossom end holds the wick, which becomes the apple's stem in the finished candle. (Both photos by Joe De Caro)

1. Open on the seam lines into two halves.
2. Remove the flat area at the bottom (the bottom or feet or whatever the toy rests on).
3. Grease the inside of both halves well.
4. Fasten the wick securely in place on top of the outside of the mold.
5. Draw the wick down the center inside the mold and out at the base.
6. Bind both halves together with tape. Tape the squeaker if it hasn't been removed, as it could leak.
7. Stand the bound toy on its top in a water glass. Place at least 1 inch of water in the bottom of the glass and be sure the container is large enough to support the toy when you pour the hot wax.
8. Pour the candle with shape coat and core wax. Center the wick while the wax is still fluid.

Toys don't often lend themselves to an overall color coat. Oil paint applied with a brush usually gives a more satisfactory finish. Poster paints and shoe polish can also be used.

Bottles

Candles for party favors are sometimes made in bottle shapes, to imitate glass bottles of perfume or a beverage. These are fun to give—and receive. Carefully remove the label of the bottle you wish to duplicate. Keep the label in the best possible condition.

If you can find a plastic bottle of similar size and shape, use it. If not you have two choices. The safest, most professional way to make a bottle candle is to remove the bottom of the bottle, using a glass cutter. Smooth the sharp edges with an emery board. You now have a mold you can use for hundreds of candles.

If you'd rather not get involved in cutting glass, pour the wax into the bottle. When the wax is firm, place the wax-filled bottle in a paper bag and give it a sharp blow with a hammer. Use gloves. Be sure all the pieces of glass are removed from the candle.

Study your bottle to see how you will insert a wick. If you plan to destroy the bottle to remove the candle you may have a wide enough neck to use a well dipped wick dropped from your wick holder into the bottle or you may finish the candle and then use a heated wick wire to pierce the wax and insert

Bottle candles are fun to make. You can use any kind of bottle you like. (Photo by Joe De Caro)

the wick. Chunky plastic bottles can have a hole placed center bottom and the wick drawn out the neck. This is more difficult to do with long or narrow necked bottles.

If you remove the bottom of a plastic or glass bottle you can use the bottle top for a wick holder. A very short (or shortened) hairpin will hold the wick in a cork. Remove the paper disc inside a metal or plastic cap, poke a hole in the center of the disc, push the wick through the hole and replace the paper disc in the bottle cap. Wedge the wick between the stopper and the bottle, if the bottle has a glass stopper.

If you are pouring a candle in a bottomless bottle, the upside-down bottle should be supported by a tin can (bend the can to fit the bottle if you need to) filled with warm water. You may find the bottle top leaks a bit but if the can is clean the wax can be dried and reclaimed.

Once the candle is free of the bottle make sure it stands without wobbling.

Now take the label you've saved and slide it through a coat of transparent wax. Before the wax has a chance to cool and dry, place the label on the candle in the appropriate place.

Spheres

Round candles are pretty and not hard to make. The procedure is a bit different, being a combination of techniques.

To create a snowball, start with an empty eggshell, a round bowl, or two halves of a child's ball.

The length of the wick is dependent on the size you want the finished candle to be and the size of the center you are using. For tiny spheres you can use a pullet egg, but regular eggs or even duck, goose, and turkey eggs can be used when they are available and suitable. The candle size can also be varied by the quantity of solid wax you dip on the egg or the amount of froth covering the outside of the solid wax. Use a wick that is at least 2 inches longer than the diameter of the entire candle you plan on making. Thus, a 1½-inch pullet egg can be dipped into a 6-inch-diameter ball and should begin with 8 inches of wick.

If you use an eggshell, drain the egg from the large end of the shell and make as small a hole as possible. Prop the shell in an empty egg carton. Pour the wax in through the opening in the shell. The wick is usually inserted with

An egg makes a fine candle. This was a duck egg and the flowers were added with an eye dropper. (Photo by Joe De Caro)

a wick wire. When the wax is solid peel off the eggshell. Dip the wax egg in as many layers of wax as you wish, until the candle is round and of a pleasing size.

Each time you dip the sphere and remove it, place it on a flat cool surface to develop a flat bottom. In the beginning you may have to hold or support the wick until the wax cools but after a few dips the bottom will enlarge enough to let the candle sit unsupported.

Next dip the sphere in shape coat to within one inch of the wick. Don't use shape coat on that top inch. The shape coat should be heavy so use cooled wax and dip several times, until the shape coat is ⅛- to ¼-inch thick, or even thicker, depending on the size of the candle.

Again rest the candle between dips on a flat surface unless you wish to design a special base for your sphere. If you do wish a special base you might consider some of the bases discussed in this book.

These candles, when they burn properly, burn quite differently from most candles. Fire burns up. The wick should use the inch of wax surrounding it (which you didn't dip in the shape coat) and then start sinking below the shape-coated outer shell of the sphere. The core wax will burn away slowly and usually the shape coat and whatever else is on the outside will remain in the form of a shell.

As the flame sinks out of sight it will also sink below the oxygen level. When you reach the point where the burning is jeopardized by the lack of oxygen put the candle out (you may not need to do this—lack of oxygen will smother the flame) and let the candle cool until it is comfortable to handle.

Use a wick wire, or a knitting needle, well heated, and pierce the outer shell of the candle. Some chandlers pierce from the inside of the candle shell to the outside but most pierce from the outside, through the decorations and shape coat into the inner cavity. Your holes need not be large or conspicuous but they should allow air, and its oxygen content, to reach the wick of the candle. If you pierce at an angle of about 45 degrees, with the low point on the outside of the candle, the holes will be hardly noticeable. Pierce from just below the melted wax level to just above to put the air where the wick most needs it and to prevent liquid wax from seeping out.

Sometimes the life of these candles is prolonged by a new wick. Pouring in a new core of wax is very impractical because the shell distorts or collapses.

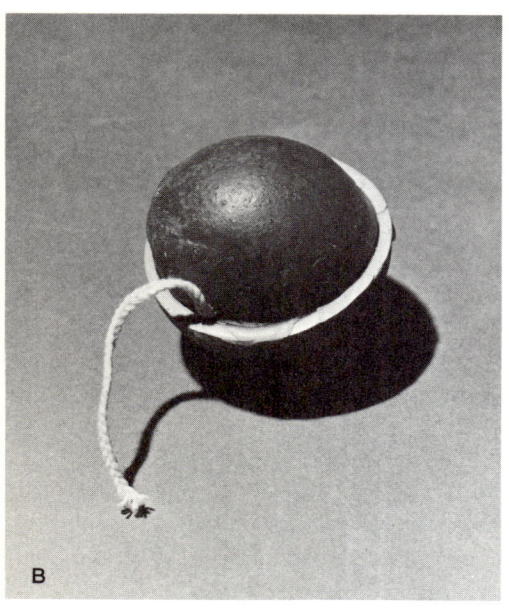

(Above) Ball-shaped candles can be made with the halves of a child's rubber ball. Here the two halves are ready to be joined.

(Above left) The halves in "A" show that the wax shrinks into a hollow center. In "B" one half is placed back inside the ball, a bit of hot wax is poured into the shrinkage hollow and the other half of the candle is placed on top to seal the two halves together.

(Left) After the halves are sealed to one another the ball is dipped until the seam disappears. S t the ball on a flat surface after each dip to make sure you develop a flat bottom. The candle is now ready to have its wick cut back and to be used as is or it can be made larger by further dipping. It could also be covered with froth.
(Photos by Joe De Caro)

But you can use a votive candle or insert a birthday candle while there is still some core wax left to support it. Cooking oil can also be used for fuel, as well as cigarette lighter fluid or some of the fluids used for colonial lamps. Lighter and lamp fluid can be perfumed if you'd like.

Using bowls and rubber balls, you can make larger ball-shaped candles than with eggs. Sometimes these are poured hollow and used with votive candles inside. If you plan to use a votive candle, cut away enough of the shell so you can lift it easily over the lighted candle; also allow an opening above the flame for the heat to escape. Without these two openings you will find it very difficult to light or snuff the inner candle and the shell could melt into a lump from trapped heat.

Examine your bowl carefully. Many bowls are not internally shaped to form a globe. The bowl should be rounded, not flat, at the bottom as well as on the sides.

(Below left) This candle, made by a seven-year-old boy, still shows a trace of the seam where the two parts of wax, molded in a bowl, were joined to one another. The child was thrilled and his mother had an added thrill on Mother's Day.
(Photo by Joe De Caro)

(Below right) Another small boy made this candle in a bowl. He especially liked carving the pattern. (Photo by Joe De Caro)

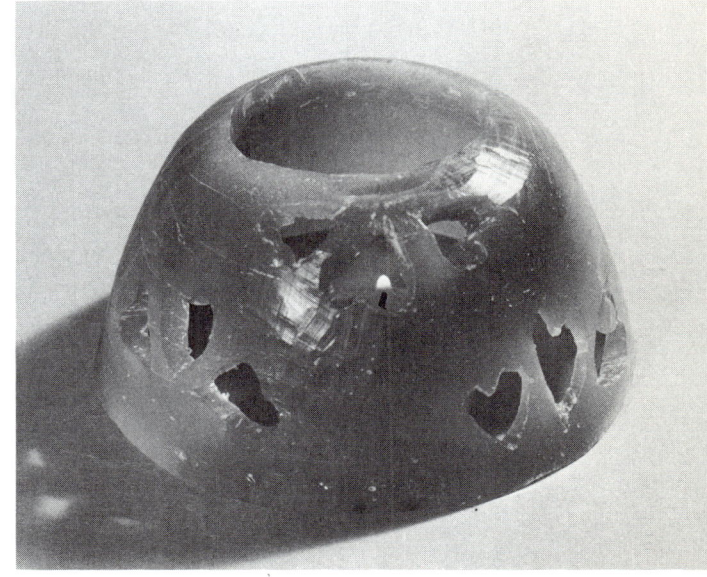

76 | The Candlemaker's Primer

Be sure to mix enough wax to allow you to pour the bowl full twice. Since you will empty the fluid wax and use only the shell, two pourings will use about 1½ bowls full (you'll have wax left over, but you need this much to pour). A solid candle will need a bit more than 2 full bowls of wax so you can successfully bond the two sections together.

Prepare about 2 pounds of wax for a 1-pint bowl and 3 pounds of wax for a 1-quart bowl. You'll use some of the wax when you pour the first bowlful. Pour in layers for a solid candle but omit the center layers for a votive shell. When the first half is finished begin on the second half.

When you make hurricane globes it is usually easier to stack one bowl-shaped shell on top of the other. If you want a solid candle the project is a bit easier to cope with if you join the two halves vertically and place the wick where the two units join each other.

These candles need not sit, however. They can be suspended like hanging baskets. If you use a hurricane-like globe for a votive candle you can imbed the hanger in the bottom shell of wax. In these the center seam is not joined,

Hanging candles are fun. Use hangers that are as flame-resistant and non-heat-conducting as you can find. Tie your candle twice with two strands each. It is also wise to give some consideration to where the candle might fall should the cords break. (Photo by Joe De Caro)

so the top half of the shell can be lifted away to light or snuff the candle. This top shell is pierced or cut open in such a way that the heat can escape. Sometimes the top shell is not used when the candle is burning.

You can use any hanger or hanging basket you already have.

A solid candle can also be hung and the hanger can be made as follows, but it must be dipped on after the candle is completed. To make a hanger for your candle, cut a disc from a plastic bottle (usually about 1 to 3 inches across) to fit the candle bottom. It is important to have this disc almost flat but it does not matter from which part of the bottle it is taken. Notch it at four equally spaced points on the outside rim. Poke a hole in the center and insert a wire-cored wick. Take two lengths of cotton yarn, cord, or leather thongs. The length is governed by the height of the hanging bracket; I suggest at least 1½ yards for each cord.

Cross these cords under the plastic disc. Fasten the cord in the notches. Pour a small puddle of wax in the center bottom of the bowl you are using for a mold and place the disc with the cords attached over the puddle. When the puddle is solid pour the bowl full of wax. Keep the cords against the sides of the bowl straight up from the notches. Fasten the excess cord to the outside of the bowl with a bit of tape so it doesn't get in the way when you empty the wax from the bowl.

From here on the shell of wax is treated like any other. If you wish to color the candle just hold the shell by the excess cord and replace it in the bowl for support until it is firm. Two or three dips and the cords will begin to look as if they are growing out of the shell.

If the bowl is large enough, instead of a votive candle you may wish to use what my studio refers to as a "wick" candle. It isn't necessarily decorative but it does burn about three times as long as a votive candle, and that can be an asset.

Use a small frozen juice can and pour a candle of core wax. It can be colored or not. You can add fragrance, and most of the time you will want to. This candle gives a good long burning time on all the hurricane types of shells that are large enough to use it.

Some bowls flare out at the top. Try making them into hanging candles, taking full advantage of that flare. They can be burned without a top half and are beautiful strung about the patio on a summer evening. Since they weigh so little they can be hung from branches or shrubs. If you use a votive candle you can add citronella or another insect repellent—just pour it into the shell on a level with the top of the candle wax. Don't get the wick wet.

9

Dipping Techniques

The aristocrats of the candle world are dipped. When man learned to dip a wick into a vat and come up with a candle, he took an exciting step forward on his pathway to light.

Dipped candles have remained the preferred choice of many people. When they are properly made they burn with a brighter, clearer, more even light than poured candles.

Our colonial foremothers used to "feather" their dipped candles by plunging them into very hot water and then shaking them dry. This changes the pore structure of the outer wax and helps the candle burn more evenly. It also helps to prevent dripping. Today we frequently expect the wax formula to take care of these problems. Feathering, however, can be very useful in some techniques.

The wax formulas for dipped candles may differ a bit from poured candles. Some craftsmen prefer to dip the entire candle in colored wax. Many craftsmen prefer to make the entire candle out of a wax that is harder than what is used for core wax, but softer than shape-coat wax.

In the studio, we usually use for dipping a formula with 60 percent paraffin and 40 percent stearic acid. Even then, we are likely to add a shape coat if the candle is to be used in warm weather. The wax of any candle should not melt

Using a homemade dipping rack, you can dip pairs of tapers which are different lengths by planning ahead and balancing your dipping rack.

Long tapers, here, are joined at the wick and dipped full length. The shorter tapers are attached to clothespin holders and dipped simultaneously. You'll coat the clothespins with wax but your dipped candles will all have the same diameter and be completed at the same time. (Photo by Joe De Caro)

until it is 10 to 20 degrees hotter than the temperature of the atmosphere to which it is exposed.

Basically, all dipped candles are either tapers or cylinders. The taper is always dipped from the same end. A cylinder is dipped by inserting the wick in the vat from alternate ends.

Sometimes a taper doesn't gain enough weight on the bottom to reach pleasing proportions. To solve this problem and to keep the candle smooth looking, dip the candle to three-quarters of its length, then dip to full length, dip to half the length and again to full length. Now dip to a quarter of the length, and so on. Keep dipping partial dips alternated with full dips, until the shape of your candle pleases you. Always end with a full dip to give your candle a smooth, well-crafted appearance.

Be sure the wax in the vat is at least 3 inches deeper than the length the finished candle is to be. Also be sure that the wax level is about 5 inches below the top of the vat. Dip the entire length of the candle. The cooler the wax, the heavier the coat of wax you will build up. The average candle will require forty to sixty dips. Have extra wax formulated and in fluid form to add to your vat if the bottom of the candle approaches the bottom of the vat when you dip.

In the chapter on equipment, you will find an explanation and directions for making a dip rack (or wick dip). You will need one dip rack for a set of tapers and two for a set of cylinders. Although I have watched craftsmen dip excellent cylinders from only one end, this seems to be a skill acquired only with much practice.

Most of the time candlemakers who dip cylinders start dipping by holding the wick at the bottom of the candle. If the candle stays cylindrical they have no problem, but if the top of the candle gets out of shape they turn the candle over, holding the wick at the top of the candle, and dip the candle back into shape.

I have seem some people change dip racks from top to bottom with every dip. Others, rather than constantly changing racks on the partially dipped candles, dip the bottom rack into the wax along with the candles, and vice versa. This leaves both dip racks as thickly coated with wax as the candles. It creates quite a cleaning project.

To clean tools or dipping racks—and they do need it periodically (espe-

Once you decide you enjoy dipping candles you'll want a studio dipping rack. This small one, electrically controlled, is a practical size for beginners. The candles on the right were dipped in a well-mixed but somewhat cool wax. This "bumpy" texture is quite pretty dipped in either the same color or a contrasting color.
(Photo by Joe De Caro)

Dipping Techniques | 83

Larger dipping racks are available from candle supply studios. (Photo by Joe De Caro)

cially just before you use them on pure white candles)—drop them in an empty vat, cover with water, and heat the water. As the wax melts it will rise to the surface of the water. If the water completely cleans the tools, you can let the vat cool and peel off the wax from the surface of the water before you lift the clean tools out.

You may wish to finish the bottom of your hand-dipped candles by slicing them with a very sharp knife when you finish dipping. Remove any extra wick and any weights at this time.

Not all candle dippers use weights, but some do to guarantee that the wick remains absolutely straight for the first few dips. These weights can be removed any time the craftsman wishes after they have served their function.

Check to see if your candle sits absolutely straight. If it will not sit straight the best way to level it is to take a table knife, heat the blade, and rub the blade back and forth on the candle bottom. Then set the candle on something flat and cool. If you have too much wax to level in this manner, rub the candle bottom back and forth over a piece of window screen. Sometimes the candle chips a bit or shows finger prints. To remedy this, once the candle stands perfectly level, give it one quick dip. After redipping hang your candle by the wick or place it immediately in a candlestick to hold it upright while it cools.

You can custom-fit candles to odd-sized candlesticks while you dip. Just dip and try on for size until the candle fits the holder, then dip once more, since the wax usually shrinks during aging.

If you want the socket to be smaller than the finished candle, dip the candle just until it fits the socket-well. Then take a piece of tape about $\frac{1}{8}$-inch narrower than the depth of the socket and bind the end of the candle. Finish dipping until the candle is the size you want it. With a sharp knife, scrape the wax at the bottom back to the tape. Remove the tape, dip once more, and you have a perfect fit.

Sometimes, especially with longer candles, making the socket separately is the answer. For the first few dips that extra inch needed for the socket causes no trouble, but when the candle is extra long, and starts nearing the bottom of the vat, your arm needs to be extra long too to keep the candle straight as you lift it in and out of the vat.

Dipping Techniques | 85

You could, as one craftsman did, climb one step up on a step ladder for every dip. But it is easier to make your socket separately, as follows:

Dip your candle until you reach the desired thickness. Grease the socket-well. Poke three or four straight pins into the bottom of the candle. Pour the socket-well completely full of liquid wax. Now sit your candle, with the pinheads into the socket-well, on the fluid wax. Hold in place until the wax solidifies.

Another method is to pour wax into the socket-well, wait until the wax begins to solidify, then insert the pins head-down into the socket-well. When the pins are held firm, dip the end of the candle in hot fluid wax and immediately force the candle onto the pin points.

This second method is most successful when you change your mind after a candle has been completed. With careful craftsmanship the candle can be complete and totally aged and still fitted to a particular holder.

It's a good idea to keep a stock of white dipped candles on hand. You can always dip them in a color coat, even two hours before a party.

Just because all dipped candles are made by the same process, there is no reason why they should lack interest. Many variations are possible. Included in this chapter are only a few. After you try the following you'll think of many more that will result in your own exclusive designs.

1. Pour a thin layer of wax on your cookie sheet. Remove a strip about ¾-inch wide and as long as you'd like a finished candle. Lay a wick carefully down the center of the strip and drool some fluid wax over this wick with your baster. Carefully place an identical strip of wax on top. Now you have a sandwich with the undipped wick and fluid wax in the center.

With your fingers, smooth out the trapped air and any excess oozing wax. Allow the fluid wax to seal the slices into one unit but don't wait until the wax is firm.

Start twisting. Some people allow the wax to hang by the wick. Most work flat on the table top. I prefer to work flat on the table top in front of a straight edge. Carefully twist your sandwich over and over and over, until the spiral pleases you. Use it as a base for dipping a cylinder. The spiral pattern will remain.

2. Dip a cylinder in several different colors of wax, one color over another.

Carve a pattern from layer to layer. This can resemble a totem pole with vivid colors and bold design, or a patchwork quilt with subtle colors and delicate designs. I've also seen such a candle used to match a pair of tapestry drapes.

3. Stripe a candle by using narrow strips of adhesive tape over the base color. The strips can be attached vertically, horizontally, or diagonally. Dip the candle in a second color of wax and peel off the tape before the top wax becomes rigid. Or leave the tape on, and place other tape over it in a cross pattern. Dip again. Now remove both tapes.

Your non-candle-making friends will go wild trying to decide how you did this.

4. Wind a soft candle with twine. Unwind a section and look. If the twine pattern isn't imbedded deeply enough you need to wind tighter.

Put on protective gloves. Dip twine, or cotton yarn, in colored wax or oil paint and wind it around another candle. The process may be messy but the results are delightful.

Put the twine on in an open pattern. Dip as you did your striped candle. The texture plus color will be lovely.

Starting your twine winding can be a problem. You can dip the end of the twine in liquid wax, place it at the bottom of the candle and work gently from there, but this can come undone. Reinforce the end with adhesive tape. You can also stick a small pin through the twine into the candle.

5. Use an eyedropper. Place your candle in a candle holder and drip a second color of wax on your candle. If the wax is quite cool it will bunch up and look like melted wax cascading down the side of a bottle. If you work with hot wax the spill will even out and you'll get some lovely running color effects.

Pick up your candle. Use an eyedropper with hot wax and turn the candle (held almost horizontally) while the wax runs.

Hold your candle on the bias and use cooler wax. With skill, using an eyedropper, you can create a trellis for tiny flowers.

6. Dip your candle in one color of cool wax. Quickly dip in a second color of hot wax. Use a comb with wide teeth and comb through the top color into the bottom color. If your hands aren't steady comb in a wiggly line.

Dip in one color. Roll the candle in kitty litter. Dip in a second color. Carefully pick out the kitty litter for an irregular, two-toned effect.

Dipping Techniques | 87

If you'd rather decorate candles than make your own, use commercial tapers. This ordinary white candle was dipped in grass green wax with pearlite floating on top. (Photo by Joe De Caro)

Dip a dark-colored candle. Use a toothpick dipped in white wax and place polka dots on the candle. The size of the dots depends on which end of the toothpick you use. The wide end of a sandwich pick will make larger dots. If you consistently dip the toothpick to the same depth in the vat you'll have all the dots the same size.

If your dots don't seem to be sticking as tightly as you'd like, touch the spots on the candle with a heated ice pick.

Improperly fastened dots may fall off after several days. Again heat is the answer. I've seen one candlemaker run very hot water from her faucet over the candle and pat the dots back into place. Next she sprayed the candle with hair spray. I prefer using a small brush and very hot wax. A touch of hot wax from the brush bristles will reseal the fallen polka dots.

7. There are a vast number of things a candle can be rolled in. Each will contribute a different look. Grate some wax. Roll a very warm, soft candle in the "coconut." You may have to use an eyedropper to drip wax in strategic spots to keep the trim where you need it.

Try shaving wax of different colors and roll the candle in these. The candle

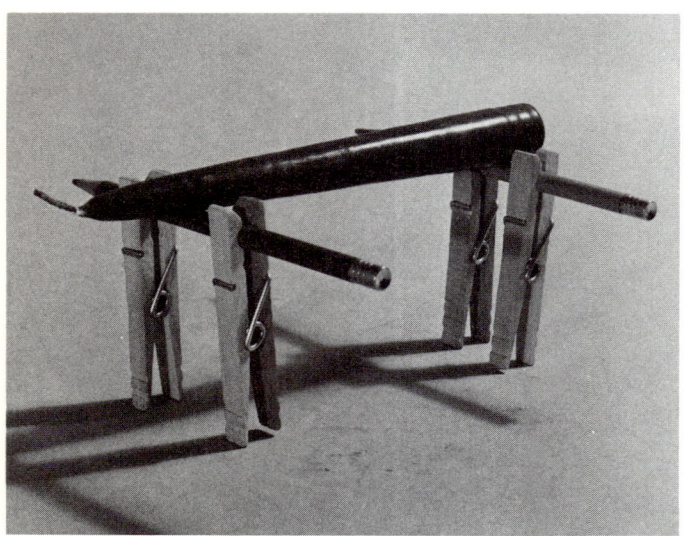

If you are placing decorations on all sides of a candle it is difficult to hold onto the candle or to place it on your workbench without distorting your decorations. Make small sawhorses using lead pencils and clip-type clothespins. These will support the candle until the decorations are attached firmly enough to move it. (Photo by Joe De Caro)

may not pick up the shaved wax but the pieces will texture the candle surface. Roll your candle on a textured fabric, metal screen, a straw place mat.

Coffee grounds, sand or pasta (especially small alphabet macaroni), sequins and glitter, either alone or together make for interesting surface effects. Multicolored glass bits, very tiny sea shells, clean fish scales (these can be tinted with a bit of food color but are beautiful alone) will each change an ordinary candle into a decorative delight.

Don't forget that the part of the candle that goes into the socket will work better without decorations and the ½ inch around the wick will burn better if left untrimmed.

Rolling your candle may present the problem of undecorated spaces where the decorations refuse to stick. Make yourself a pair of small sawhorses by clamping a lead pencil between two clip clothespins. Rest the ends of the candle on these. With the candle suspended thus you can use an eyedropper to add a drop of hot wax exactly where you want it and get the decorations into place without fear of injury to the other side of the candle.

8. Shave a bit of colored wax from each of several crayons. Place the crayon shavings on waxed paper or aluminum foil and warm the crayon shavings to the melting point. A warm oven or radiator will work well, and a hostess tray will also do a fine job. You may wish to place the waxed paper on your cookie sheet.

Your colors can be placed helter-skelter or you can plan a pattern of stripes, or control colors for a tweed look. Be sure the colors are in proper relationship before you heat them. When the crayon melts roll a white or pastel candle over the sheet of chips.

This is a vivid color treatment. Rolled across, the candle will have an all-over pattern. If you place the colors in stripes the candle will have color stripes. Slide your candle slowly up and down as you roll it across and the colors will marbleize.

9. Let any leftover color from the above technique become firm. Peel it from the wax paper, toss it on top of a dipping vat containing white or pale colored wax. Dip a candle through the color. No two candles dipped in this vat will look alike. As the candles carry the color deeper and deeper into the vat and the colors melt, you will find each new candle is dipped with a softer, more blended finish.

90 | The Candlemaker's Primer

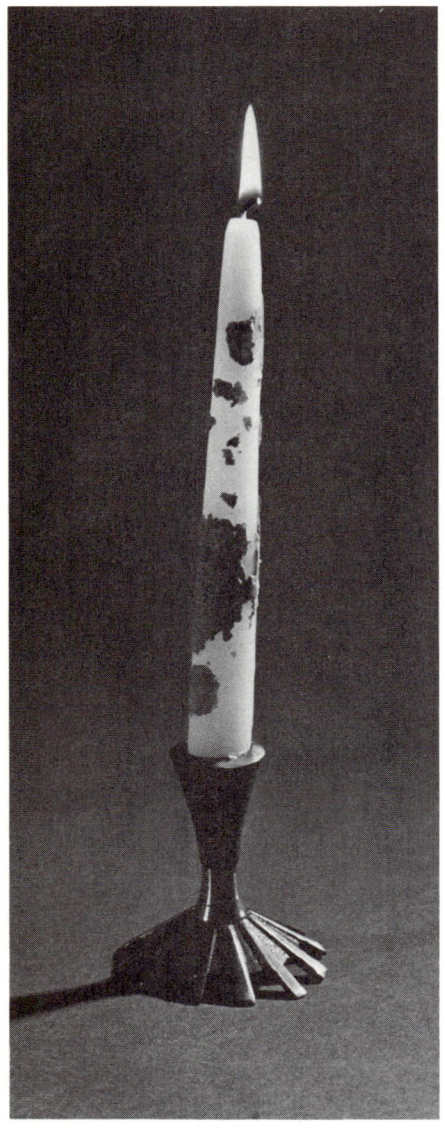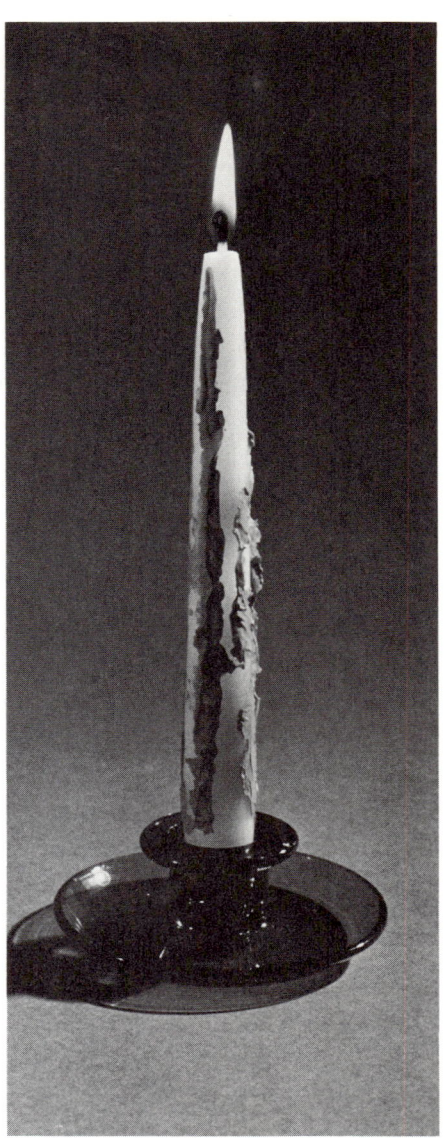

You can come up with an unusual color pattern by rolling a warm candle over melted, shaved, or grated bits of crayon (candle at left). If you slide the warm candle straight up or down on the color, you get a three-dimensional striped pattern (candle at right). (Photos by Joe De Caro)

10. Pour a bit of bright-colored wax into a vat of pale-colored wax. Don't stir but dip quickly. Candles will be marbleized. Leftovers from this vat can be stirred together to make a solid-color wax.

11. Dip a candle full length into a vat containing a pastel color. Stop here and decide how many shades of this color you wish and where you want the colors to deepen on your candle. Mark the candle. Add more pigment to the vat. Stir well. Dip again to just above the mark. Mark the candle for the next dip. Add still more color to the vat. Stir well and dip again.

If you continue this procedure you will have a candle whose colors blend from the dark bottom to light top (or vice versa). If you are dipping many candles, mix a vat for each shade. Placing the vats in a row, start at one end and dip the candles from vat to vat. If the color contrast lacks subtlety try a quick dip in a vat of very hot water to blend the shades together. Make sure the water is very hot, so that you blend the wax and dip as quickly as possible.

12. Café candles that drip in many colors are always fascinating. The secret ingredient is in the wick. Thread a length of undipped wick through a large-eyed needle. Chop hunks of kindergarten crayons and thread these on the wick. Don't force the crayon pieces tightly together; leave a bit of room for formulated wax to reach the wick. Now dip your candle as usual. Unless this candle is going to be exposed to extreme heat, omit the shape coat to encourage the wax to run. If you use a shape coat cut through it in several places to start the wax running.

13. Dipped candles can also be used for imitation sculpture. Long, tall figurines can be extremely austere or very whimsical. Foliage and flowers can be imitated. You can model these as you would sculpture while the wax is still slightly warm.

Dip a taper in yellow wax. Score it both horizontally and vertically until the whole surface is checkered with a multitude of small pillows. Dip some fibers of cotton batting or fishbowl filter in tan wax and place these near the top of the taper. Wrap some oblongs of green sheet wax around the bottom two-thirds of the taper. Presto, an ear of corn!

Your imagination sets the limit to the number and type of creations you can dip from your candle vat.

10

Candle-Crafting

You have mastered the techniques of making wicks and formulating wax. You have poured and dipped and been pleased with what you have accomplished. This leaves crafting to put some love into your creations. Here is where you express your personality, where you make your very own mood candle.

Techniques vary from simple cookie-cutting to assembling a number of parts, such as for a floating flower for a dining table centerpiece. A tall stacked candle may call for the loving care of the sculptor or the design skill of an architect.

Sheet Wax

The most versatile materials for crafting are thin sheets of wax ($1/16$- to $1/2$-inch thick). This thickness of the sheet is frequently important. Make a simple measuring gauge by piercing a pencil eraser with a corsage pin or long needle. Place the pin upright with the point touching the bottom of the sheet of wax. Move the eraser down until it rests on the wax. Move the gauge to different places on the sheet of wax. Is the entire sheet the same thickness? Do you want to work with thick wax or thin wax?

Formulas for sheet wax usually call for core wax plus color. When the design requires a very soft, easily shaped wax or a more transparent wax, the

Flowers make an excellent project for students who enjoy craft techniques.

Plant a taper in a flower pot filled with plaster or sand. Shape a flower at the top. The leaves can be cut from beeswax, as shown, or from a thin sheet of colored candle wax. If you like the natural curve of the stem, use no shape coat and work the flower petals into place immediately after you finish dipping the candle. Place in a candlestick to cool. Watch it carefully so the "stem" doesn't curve too much.

Votive candles can also be wrapped in flower petals to make pretty additions to foliage arrangements. (Photo by Joe De Caro)

94 | The Candlemaker's Primer

quantity of paraffin in the formula is increased. You can also use the sheets of beeswax that are sold in candle-craft shops.

If you work with what amounts to a paraffin-plus-color formula, be sure the area surrounding the wick is protected by a slower burning wax.

Ask yourself where you intend to use your candle. No one would want to get up from the dinner table to restoke a candle. A candle that could burn for only a short time would be much easier to manage at a tea table or party buffet with people constantly moving about. Be sure the candle you design will burn as long as you need.

Floating Candles

Floating candles are the least seen of the commercial candles. They don't pack or ship well and won't survive much handling by customers, so the average candle shop doesn't stock them. You can make some as a group project or on your own. Use any commercial paper flower patterns if you wish to start with flower candles. Cut the sheet wax just as if it were paper. You

Floating candles are always a delight. This one, designed for a birdbath (after dark when the birds aren't bathing), will brighten up a garden party. The extra leaf can be used to float a real flower. (Photo by Joe De Caro)

can also use origami patterns this way, or use children's paper cutout books for patterns.

The problem with a floating candle is to provide enough fuel to keep the candle burning. Sometimes, with a flower candle, you can shape the stamen area like a small cup and insert the wick in the center. Perhaps the flower will need other wick-like additions just to look like a flower. These can be placed around the outer edge of the cup. When it comes time to burn this candle, first fill the cup with cooking oil.

When you make a floating candle, keep a bowl of water nearby and test each layer of wax as well as each additional piece of wax as you add it. If the candle starts to sink you must increase the surface area of wax on the water.

For example: try a 2-inch square of $\frac{1}{8}$-inch thick wax. The points of the square may be shaped like petals. Leave the center solid but shape it like a cup if you desire. Work from a flat surface in the center up and out and have the edge turned up a bit. Work slowly and gently. Allow the warmth of your fingers to penetrate the wax. Study the way the petals and center curve on living flowers.

If this is a daisy, or another flower with a single layer of petals, make only the center section. On a more complex flower, add additional layers of leaves and petals.

Test the base petals in a bowl of water. Be sure they float level to the top of the water. If they sink low, add leaves in a balanced pattern. If they sink more on one side than the other, add one or more extra leaves on the low side. Place the first leaf at the low spot. Flowers usually don't look well if more than two-thirds surrounded by leaves. If the flower still isn't floating on top of the water, place the other leaves where they seem to be needed.

If leaves don't keep the candle from sinking, try adding a stem, a part of a flower, or a bud, or follow the directions for doughnuts (below).

When your flower is balanced and floating well, seal the leaves or other flower sections with a drop of fluid wax so the pieces become a single unit.

The center section with the stamen is next. Take a piece of warm wax the size of a marble and shape it into a deep cup by working it over the end of your finger or a round handle. Be sure the very bottom is flat to help the cup fasten to the petal section. If necessary, tap the cup against the table top to flatten it.

Now with an eyedropper drip some colored wax, one drop at a time, over the lip of the cup to imitate stamens. Whenever possible have the wax flow down the outside of the cup. Place the eyedropper in the center of the cup and make a puddle with a drop or two of wax. Insert a well-dipped wick about 2 inches long, and support the wick until the wax hardens.

When the wick is steady float your petals on the bowl of water. Add your stamen section. If the petals tip try sliding the stamens a bit to see if you can correct the balance.

Look at your flower critically. Does it look exactly as you want it to? You can use a toothpick dipped in wax to make markings or grate a bit of wax onto the center for additional stamens.

When the flower is finished the last thing to do is to drop some liquid wax in the center of the petal section and place the stamen section on the puddle to fuse them into a unit.

Floating flowers are beautiful but other life forms can also be used. Swans, turtles, and frogs are great fun.

Since water evaporates and can leave a visible ring around a bowl, try not to leave your candles floating in water for extended periods of time.

Shampoos, dish detergents, and household cleaning liquids frequently come in lovely colors. Add the milder smelling fluids for a wonderful background.

Cookie-cutter shapes can make fine floating candles. Use them as they come from the cutter, with a birthday-candle wick in the center. Flower-shaped wax cupcakes also make lovely floating candles. These are frequently used for the wick section of giant candles to float on swimming pools. Be sure you float pool candles on cork or blocks of wood to keep melted wax out of the pool filter.

DOUGHNUTS: Any time you have leftover sheet wax, cut a doughnut. These are the darlings of floating arrangements and as useful under fresh flowers as they are under candles. You can use many sizes and not all need to have holes. Actually these doughnuts are discs of wax which frequently have the centers removed; hence the name. Cut them in a variety of sizes with kitchen bottle tops and slip them under a blossom or candle to help it float. Always use the largest possible doughnut that can be safely hidden. It helps to match the color of the doughnut to whatever it supports. If one large doughnut doesn't do the job, or isn't large enough, two or three small ones can be used.

Candle-Crafting | 97

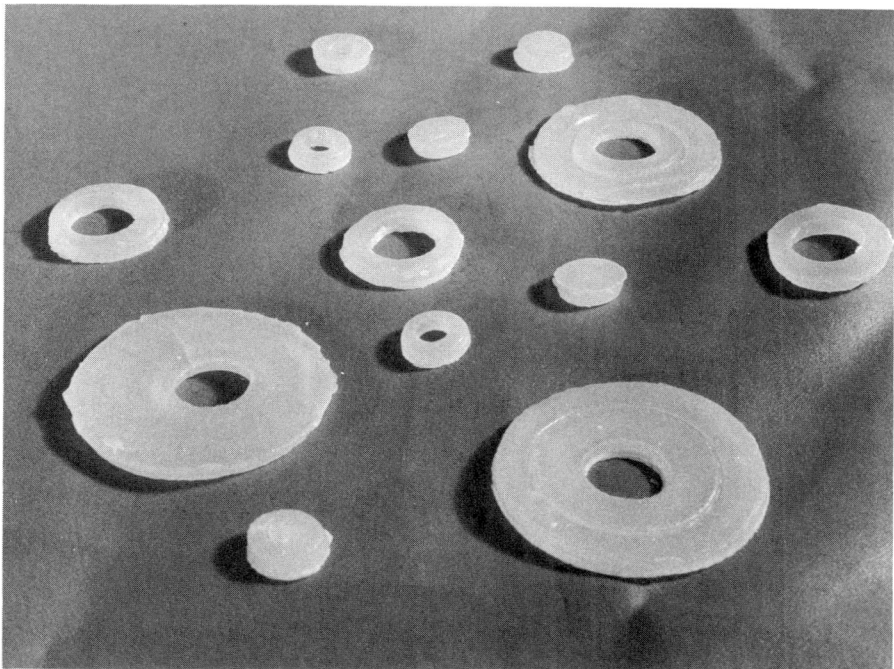

Wax doughnuts should be many sizes and shapes. Cut them from scraps of sheet wax. These are used to help flower blossoms float or to buoy up your candles. (Photo by Joe De Caro)

Twists

Sheet wax can be used for twisted candles. Pour a sheet of wax about ⅜-inch thick. Stretch undipped wicking from one edge of the sheet to the other, as straight as possible, in parallel rows at intervals of 3 inches or more. It helps if the wick has been given one quick dip in wax but it should not be dressed as it normally would be. Secure each wick by dripping a column of wax from your baster along its length. Now pour another layer of wax the full size of the cookie sheet. This can be the same color as the first layer, or a

The twisted candle can be a graceful addition to your decor. This twisted taper is called a charm candle because it twists only twice. (Photo by Joe De Caro)

different color. Cut the wax between the wicks as soon as the second sheet of wax has become opaque. Each slice should be 2 to 3 inches wide.

Lift a slice of wax containing a wick from the cookie sheet. Lay it flat on the work surface and rub the edges with your fingers until the two layers of wax fuse into one unit; if necessary use a hot knife for this job. Don't allow either the sheet of wax or the slice of wax to become cold or rigid.

Let the slice of wax rest on the workbench as you turn it over and over until the twist pleases you. The completely twisted candle is called a spiral. One or two revolutions make a charm candle; three or four make what is referred to as a hunting candle.

The square, abrupt top may need to be reshaped to be more esthetically pleasing. Use a sharp knife to cut the wax. Follow a pattern so both sides are shaped the same. This is especially important if you are making a pair or more of matching candles. The pattern can be extremely simple.

Cut an arc that pleases you from a piece of scrap paper. Use the pattern on one side for the right side of the candle, then turn it over and use it for the left.

Handle the bottom in much the same manner. Make a pattern with a gradual curve. Cut the sides to match. Fit the candle to a candlestick. If the candle does not fit properly, follow the directions for making separate candle bottoms given on page 85.

Keeping a twisted candle straight is a bit tricky. Using a plumb line while the candle is still soft is the best guide. Place your candle under a light fixture, a clothesline, or anything that you can tie a wick to. Tie one end of a raw wick or string to the clothesline or light fixture. Weight the other end with a heavy washer or anything similar that will force the cord to hang straight. Match your twisted candle to this line.

Another method sometimes used with twisted candles is to tie the wick of the candle at the top and let the wick weight dangle from the bottom of the candle.

Sandwich Candles

Some paraffin or household wax is packaged in slices (photo A). Candles made from these slices are always a hit with impatient students.

Use broken tapers for the wick if you wish. Shave off wax from the taper's wide end so it will be no thicker than the slice of wax. Split one slice of wax

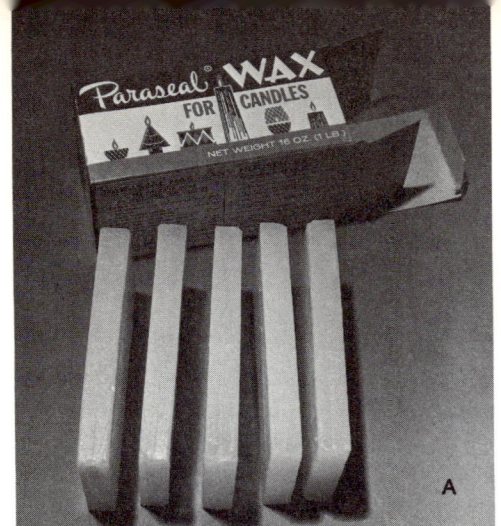

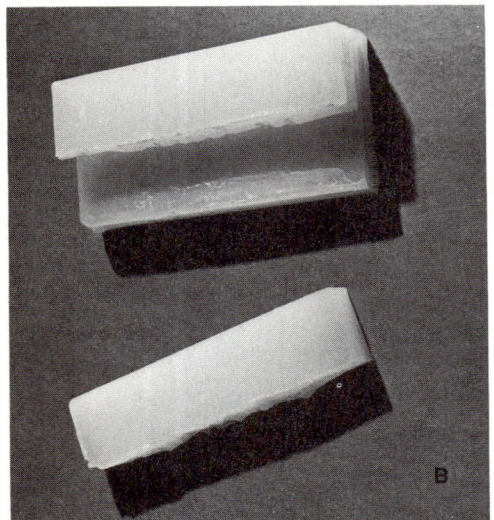

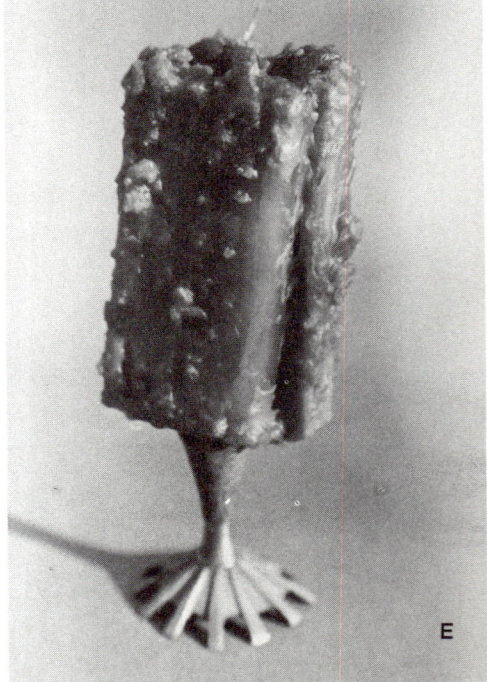

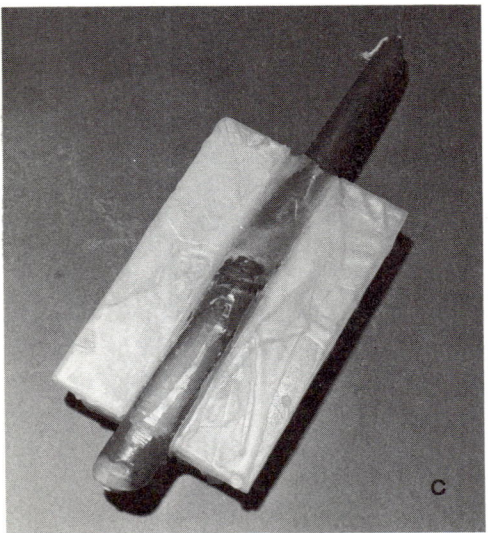

(Photos by Joe De Caro)

lengthwise and join it to the full-sized slice of wax (as in photo B). Place the taper you are using for a wick in place. Use the other half slice of wax to complete the layer and fuse the unit with melted wax (see photo C). Top with a full slice of wax.

The outer slices can be carved into ghost faces or caricatures (as in photo D). Finished without carving, the candle is chunky and irregularly shaped (see photo E). This candle was dipped in colored wax that had bits of solid wax floating through it.

Burning Bushes

Candles referred to as "burning bushes" are quite spectacular to use. I suggest you lay the pattern out on a piece of tissue paper the size and shape of your cookie sheet. Be sure to make a carbon copy.

Draw as many oblong leaves as the paper will hold. The shape of the leaf is up to you; tulip or elongated philodendron leaves are popular. You can vary the size of the leaf, as a variety of sizes is more pleasing than all one size.

When the paper pattern is completed pour a layer of leaf-colored wax into your cookie sheet. Remember that leaves have many colors and that you can take poetic license if you wish. Let the wax solidify and become opaque but not cool enough to be firm.

Mark the top of the sheet of wax and the top of each pattern piece in exactly the same place. Place the pattern on top of the wax sheet and pierce through the pattern into the wax, using a hat pin or large needle. Outline every leaf, and be sure you make visible marks. You can also mark the outlines with a number of straight pins, leaving them in the wax and gently tearing the paper away. Keep the carbon pattern handy for reference.

Lay pieces of undressed wick down the center of each leaf where the vein would be. Secure the wick with dabs of hot wax and then pour another sheet of wax over the top. This can be the same color as the first sheet of wax, or a different color. For example, some house plants have leaves with magenta tops and green undersides.

As soon as the second layer of wax is opaque and firm enough to handle, take a sharp knife and cut out each leaf. This is where the carbon copy of your pattern helps. If you are not sure of the shape of a leaf you can replace the paper pattern, using the carbon copy, and locate your mark again.

Figure 8. For a burning bush, mark pattern on wax in your cookie sheet. Assemble finished leaves or petals into a plant.

As you remove the leaves from the sheet of wax, use a tweezer to pull the wick out about ¼ inch from the tip of each leaf. Now gently shape the leaves and rub the edges lightly with your fingers until the seam line is hidden. To smooth the edges you can also dip the leaf back in hot wax, hold the edge over a candle flame, or use a brush with some hot wax.

These leaves should cup a bit and perhaps flute at the edges. The bases of the leaves are generally shaped so that they will fit into one another at the stem end.

As many leaves as you wish can be assembled into one plant. There are a variety of assembly methods. Some artists prefer to use a candlestick. Others work around a votive or wick candle.

If you'd like a small, spreading bush, with the flame quite low it is best to start with a votive candle shape (you can make this of extra burning-bush wax). Place the smallest leaves around the votive candle. As the leaves get larger shape them to curl outward. Be sure the very largest leaves have the tips with the wick pointing up.

Many times, with a center votive candle the center burns for several minutes before the rest of the bush is lit. No matter how secure your spreading bush seems, remember to place something underneath that will catch drips as the leaves burn.

For a tall bush you have two possible centers. You can work around a taper or you can simply roll the largest leaves into a tight core. The next tallest leaves are then added and so on until you have the very smallest leaves on the outside. Shape each wick tip away from the bush itself to prevent the wick from burning any leaf it is not a part of. A wick placed too close to other leaves will burn not only its own leaf but also the leaves nearby.

These candles are sometimes varied by the addition of flowers. Most paper flower patterns can be adapted to this purpose. Petals and leaves are normally of three basic shapes, with many variations; they can be twisted to conform to your project. If your leaf or petal is basically oblong, heart-shaped, or hand-shaped (sometimes open-fingered and sometimes close-fingered like a mitten) you should have no trouble designing a variety of flowers or leaves.

Froth

One of the most popular methods of decorating a candle is wax froth. Use half the usual quantity of stearic acid in your paraffin—about 20 percent of the formula—to make the wax opaque. For best results start to work with about 1 quart of wax at a time.

Let the wax cool until it has a good skin on top. Stir this and allow to set until the skin forms again. Stir again. Repeat this process until about half the wax in the vat has solidified. Now beat the wax until it is thick and frothy. You can use an egg beater, a wire whisk, or a fork. Each will give a slightly different texture. Much depends on the utensil you are accustomed to using.

Froth doesn't always have to be white or all of one color. Add color if you'd like. One very different effect comes from adding a bit of fluid dark

104 | The Candlemaker's Primer

color just before you stop beating the wax. To get the color fluid, melt a crayon with an equal amount of paraffin (use an old jar lid or something you can throw away). Stop beating when the dark color has made swirl patterns in the froth. If you beat too long, the color will blend.

Mixing froth in large batches creates a few extra problems and should be avoided unless necessary. Not the least of the problems is keeping the wax soft and pliable enough to use. An electric warming appliance with its stabilized heat is excellent, and a hot radiator will also hold a vat of froth at a good temperature for quite a while. You can also heat your oven a bit—less than 200 degrees is fine—turn it off, and place the vat of excess froth in the oven until you need it.

Use wax froth for a decorative finish on a variety of candles. It is especially useful if you have a candle whose color or finish you don't like. A visit to the candle department of a good gift boutique will give you many ideas on how froth can be used. A candle supply shop will also display froth used in a variety of ways.

Froth is as versatile as the proverbial "little black dress." Here it forms the foliage on a tree shading three little elves. The treetop, cast in a soda-fountain cup, uses the bottom of a taper as a trunk. This type of candle is inclined to be top-heavy, so it stands on "ground" of sand-colored wax poured in a small cake pan. (Photo by Joe De Caro)

A birthday centerpiece for a young child can be made by using a small plastic train for shaping birthday candles and a large froth-covered candle for the "candlestick." A second set of identical train-shaped candles might go on the real cake.
(Photo by Joe De Caro)

Try the froth as a modeling medium. Shape a snowball and insert a well-dipped wick. For a different effect wait until your ball of froth has become completely cooled and rigid. Now give the candle a quick dip in colored wax.

You can also use froth for snow masses on your Christmas tree or for other scenic decorations. If you'd like an igloo, use a small bowl and proceed as you would for pouring Indian tepees (see pages 59–60).

Sand Casting

This is a creative design process for free-form candles. It gives the designer full opportunity to create the shape, size, depth, and breadth of a candle he desires.

Select a container at least one-third larger than the finished candle you wish to make. The container for a sand-cast candle need not be something that will withstand heat, or even much moisture, but it does need to be sturdy. If heat or water might harm the container, line it with aluminum foil.

Distribute a layer of sand evenly in the bottom of the container. Two inches will be enough for an average candle, but very large candles need more and some candles, especially those less than four inches in diameter, can be cast with less.

For your beginning attempts place a smaller box or bowl in the center of the layer of sand. Now fill in the space around the bowl or box with damp sand and pat the sand until it is well packed.

Carefully remove the inner box or bowl. If any of the sand sifts out of place push it back where it belongs. You may need a bit more water to hold it in place. Use a spray bottle from a household cleaner.

When you have become more skilled you may wish to shape the sand without the help of the inner container. This is fine. The inner shape is recommended only to guarantee success at the beginning. Some casters never use it. Other casters prefer the inner container for the symmetry it gives the candle.

If you wish legs on your candle you can scoop out small holes in the bottom of the sand before you pour your candle. Usually three legs are easier to balance than four. There are a number of ways to level the legs once the candle is cast, so all you need consider is that the legs look alike before you pour.

(Top) A sand-casting container need not be something that will withstand heat, or even hold water. Here an old tub with a small leak is lined with aluminum foil.

(Left) You can use materials other than sand to cast candles. This candle was cast in a mixture of soil, peat moss, and grass seed. As you can see, the grass is beginning to grow. It might be fun to try small flower seeds with this mixture.

(Above right) Mushrooms can be either partly or entirely sand-cast. Here the top of the mushroom was cast in aquarium stone. These are top-heavy candles. Use a well-dressed wick and reinforce the base by imbedding a piece of cardboard tube in it. When the tube is completely covered with wax it helps the candle to stand alone.

(Photos by Joe De Caro)

You can vary the appearance of the outer shell of sand with the heat of the wax and the quantity of water in the sand. If you wish a sheer grainy look, keep the sand as wet as possible and pour the wax when it is as cool as it can be and still remain fluid.

If, on the other hand, you like the popular look of a sand shell all around the candle, let the sand get as dry as it can be and still hold its shape. Pour the candle with the wax as hot as possible.

If you pour over wet sand, wear long sleeves, gloves, and keep your face protected. The wax on the wet sand is likely to create a cloud of steam. On dry sand, there is not likely to be much steam, but there could be a bit of spattering if there is any foreign ingredient in the sand. A lot depends on where your sand comes from. Beach sand usually contains remnants of water insects and animals. Garden sand also contains small bits of animal life or vegetation and even the purest sand contains silica, the base material for manufacturing glass.

When pouring these candles try varying the temperature of the wax and the amount of moisture in the sand.

You can inlay other materials into the sand shells. Try some of the pretty gravel used in aquariums, small clams and other sea shells, coffee grounds, kitty litter, vermiculite, wild bird seed, pasta, beads, colored pearl or glass chips, or even wisps of the fiber glass used in fishbowl filters.

Some of these materials will hold well on wet sand but will slide to the bottom on dry sand. If they slide, use your finger or a spoon to make a ridge around the casting, forming a border or a design. Fill this ridge to the brim with the material you wish to use. Properly done, the ridge will hold the material in place.

If you use hot wax, remember that the wax will penetrate the sand to a depth of at least 1 inch to form the shell, so mix your added materials to a depth of at least 2 inches.

To make giant sand-cast candles, find something really large to hold the sand while casting. If you use an inner container, find out how much wax it will hold by measuring its dimensions or by filling it with water, 1 quart at a time, remembering that 1 quart of water represents from 2 to 2½ pounds of wax.

Decide how many wicks you wish in your candle. Many big, squat candles have more than one wick. Cast your wicks in something bigger than usual, such as a large juice can.

Some of these candles look so huge you wonder about their weight. If you are concerned about the weight of your proposed candle, you can fill the cavity with snowballs made of completely firm wax froth. These can be the same color as the candle and will create surface texture, or they can be of complementary colors. The color will melt a bit on the edges and swirl into the base color.

For a super-sized candle, melt the wax in more than one vat. You know your own strength. Can you handle 15 pounds of 190-degree wax safely? I have a candle made of 60 pounds of wax. This required four vats of wax all mixed with identical ingredients and all equally hot at the same time.

Identical color in each vat will produce a candle of one solid color. You can have a variation in color by adding different colors to different vats.

When all your wax is ready, start pouring into the center bottom of the sand. Pour steadily; don't dump. If you dump you may splash the hot wax or move the sand, which could start a slide and distort or ruin your candle.

More than one person can pour the wax. Remember to give each vat one final complete stir just before you pour. The wax from each vat should be poured into the same spot.

There are some interesting things you can achieve when more than one person does the pouring. Two people pouring a very wide candle may establish two pouring spots, but for the nicest candle the wax should spread outward and upward from a single location in an unbroken pattern.

If two people pour different colors the candle will have areas of solid color, swirled color, and mixed color. If they stand opposite one another each color will be distributed over about half the candle. Very few people coordinate with one another well enough to keep the halves completely equal. If they shift position while pouring, ending up standing next to one another, the pattern will become more or less fan-shaped. If they swap colors there will be still different effects.

When three people stand equidistant there can be a wide variety of mixed colors. If all the wax is poured into one central spot the effect will be very different than when each person pours in the center of his portion of the candle.

Six people pouring simultaneously in alternate colors produce an effect resembling peppermint candy. This can be fun on camping trips. The big candle can be used as a substitute for a bonfire on a rainy night.

Graduated Stacked Candles

For a graduated series of candles, collect empty tin cans of various sizes. You can stack them while empty and plan your tower accordingly.

Decide on the approximate height of your candle. Start building with the largest can, and add progressively smaller cans until the stack has reached its intended height. Examine the tower critically to make sure you like the proportions. Do you want the units deeper and wider, or shorter and narrower?

Once you've decided which cans to use, pour them as you would any other candle. Remove them from their molds and color coat as you prefer. Some artists like to whittle the units into one giant taper. Add your wick.

One way to decorate such a candle is to pour a thin sheet of wax on a cookie sheet. While the wax is still warm and pliable cut it into any desired pattern. In the beginning it may be easier to cut this into long strips or small

To make a tall stacked candle, you start with empty tin cans. After the sections have been poured, you can whittle them into a tower or make a trim that will cover the seams.
(Photo by Joe De Caro)

units. Accomplished craftsmen sometimes work with an entire sheet of carved wax, but this demands a lot of experience in fitting designs and patterns in addition to handling the warm wax.

Try a grille-work pattern in black over a brightly colored candle for a Spanish effect, or try reproducing the "gingerbread" seen on mid-Victorian houses. Make borders of geometric patterns like those used in ancient Greek art.

Keep the wax warm and pliable. Wrap the carved wax over the candle to cover the joints where your candle sections join one another.

Fireplace Candles

A fireplace in a modern home is frequently a luxury. It isn't just that logs are hard to obtain and expensive. In all probability the house has a good central-heating system, and heat from the fireplace upsets the thermostatic controls of the entire house.

Many people keep an arrangement of logs in the fireplace that looks ready to burst into flame at any moment. They get an actual "fire in the fireplace" effect without burning any wood. Candles are the answer.

Drill or bore holes about 2 inches wide and about 2 inches deep into the top and back logs of your arrangement. Insert candles.

This can be done in one of two ways. You can line each hole with aluminum foil and pour core wax directly into the hole. As the wax begins to thicken, insert a well-dressed wire core wick.

The second method is to pour your candles in small units such as frozen juice cans (6-ounce size). When you are ready to insert the candle, wrap the candle with aluminum foil which acts as insulation for the log. Separate candles are easily replaced but since they protrude from the log they are easier to spot, which spoils the illusion that the logs are burning in the beginning.

Burning candles instead of the logs has several advantages. There is no heat involved, and no problem of having to add another log to the fire while a party is in progress. The fragrance of the candles (try apple, cherry, walnut, or pine, or even an oriental incense) will fill the room. If you like to watch the flames and dream, treat your wicks so they burn in color.

When the candles are carefully arranged you will have all the delights of a burning fireplace, even on a hot July night.

Sculpturing

Wax will carve as easily as soap. Like alabaster, it is soft and pleasing to stroke. There are many different things that can be carved out of wax, and tools can be just as varied. A hammer and chisel are no better than whittling with a pen knife. Everything depends on the result you desire.

Carved animals can be realistic, surrealistic, or caricatures. A porcupine with small candles for each quill is most effective when burning. Garlands of flowers are unusual. Try a Della Robbia type of wreath with small candles interspersed to flicker light on the lovely design.

Hobnail Patterns

Hobnail patterns can be created much the same way as polka dots on dipped candles (see page 88). To apply hobnails, use the end of a baster or the large end of a sandwich pick. Knitting needles and cuticle sticks from manicuring equipment also work well. Some candle artisans use brushes, but it takes real skill and considerable practice to reproduce hob after hob of the same size with a brush.

Reviving Decorations

Old, tired, paper flowers can be revived by quickly dipping them in wax and shaking the excess wax back into the pot. Reshape the petals before the wax cools. Fabric flowers may be treated the same way.

Applying a non-wax decoration to a candle can usually be accomplished in one of three ways:

1. Dip the entire decoration in wax and very quickly apply the decoration to the candle.

2. Apply the flame of another candle to the spot where the decoration will look best and gently press the decoration into the melted wax.

3. Paint a bit of very hot wax on the candle with a brush and press the decoration into place.

If this bonding leaves an unfilled area, fill it in with a drop or two of fluid wax on a brush or toothpick. Any rough spots can be smoothed with warm knife blades or polished with a soft cloth. A bit of household cooking oil on the cloth is sometimes helpful.

Leftovers

Most of us hate to discard small amounts of useful materials, but there comes a time when our need for order and storage space challenges our desire for thrift.

Some of the most delightful candles can be created by combining small amounts of leftover colored wax. The colored waxes also make fine decorations for larger candles.

The maximum accomplishment in using leftovers is probably the combination of a leftover drinking glass and several bits of leftover colored wax.

Use any clean glass you have on hand. The shape of the glass will not be important since the candle can remain in the glass. A large mouth or top is important, however, since you will need to reach the wick to light it and the wick will need oxygen to burn.

Gather your bits of colored waxes and arrange them in the color sequence you prefer for a horizontally striped candle.

The wick can be placed in the glass before you pour the first layer but if you'd like to hide the bottom of the wick it can be inserted after you pour the first layer of wax. A bit of florist clay or sticky tape will hold the bottom of

You can use up many of the odd glasses in your cupboard when you use leftover wax.
(Photo by Joe De Caro)

the wick to the bottom of the glass if the wick is inserted first. When you insert the wick after the first layer of wax use a weight (a small washer or wick tab works fine). Suspend the wick from the wick holder on the top of the glass and be sure the wick is straight. Now pour the first few drops of wax around the wick very carefully to make sure it doesn't move.

Use a small vat and melt one color of wax at a time. Pour the melted wax into the glass in layers. The horizontal stripes need not all be the same width. When you feel adventuresome you can tilt the glass to get diagonal stripes or you can keep changing the position of the glass until the colored wax is wedge-shaped or chevron-patterned (see figure 9).

One small vat (a tin can is usually large enough) can be used to melt all the different colored waxes if you are careful not to mix uncompatible colors. When you have poured as much of a dark stripe as you'd like you can add some white wax to make a pastel stripe of the same basic color.

You may wish to change the color of your candle from one stripe to the next. Perhaps you wish to put a bright green stripe on top of a deep mauve stripe. To use the same vat first pour all the mauve wax from the vat. Now you can either cool the vat enough to clean it further or you can add some white wax and pour a narrow stripe of this wax.

Figure 9. When you pour stripes of colored wax into a glass you need not always have even horizontal stripes. The glass on the left was tipped to the right and the glass on the right was tipped to alternate sides for each new stripe.

The white wax will pick up any smidgin of leftover mauve-colored wax in the vat. If you were to add the bright green wax to a vat containing mauve wax, the combined colors might turn the bright green into a brown green that may not be to your liking.

Another method of using leftover colored wax is to dice the wax into cubes. Candle supply shops sell cubes of uniform size but if you cube your own wax you can cut your cubes in a variety of sizes which could make your color combination more interesting.

Select a mold or an empty glass and fasten a well-stiffened wick to the bottom. You can buy wicks with a wire core that are frequently used in this type of candle but I prefer a very well-dressed wick or even a taper. Some chandlers use a wick wire and insert the wick after the candle is completed.

Drop the assortment of colored wax cubes into the mold or glass. Pour white or contrasting colored wax over the cubes. For the prettiest candles keep the fluid wax as transparent as possible by using very little or no stearic acid in your formula. You might try a teaspoon of beeswax to a cup of candle wax.

There will be little shrinkage as the candle cools since more than half the candle is made up of the already cooled wax in the cubes. If this candle is poured with very hot wax the cubes will melt and the color will swirl. You can stir the wax to increase the swirls of color if you like. If, on the other hand, you pour this candle with cooler wax, the cubes will remain intact.

GRANULES: Another way to use leftovers is to grate or grind the colored wax. Mix the bits of colored wax with enough core wax to make a sheet of wax. When the sheet of wax is solid it can be broken up and grated or put through a meat grinder. You can also do this with small nuggets of colored wax or crayons, core wax, and shape wax.

If just one color of grated wax is used, you can layer it between cans or milk cartons of two different sizes (following directions for pouring wax over ice cubes or vermiculite, page 65). Even cool wax may cause the granules to run and swirl a bit, but a multishaded candle can be quite pretty.

You can also mix the granules in an assortment of pleasing colors and either treat as above or place them in any odd glass or small glass bowl and fill with core wax. Your glass of wax may be speckled or look like tweed.

Fasten a well-stiffened wick to the bottom of the glass. Candle supply houses sell wicks with a wire core that are frequently used in this type of candle. You can also dip your wick until it becomes stiff enough to stand alone.

I prefer to place my wick securely in the glass before I add the granules.

APPLIQUÉ: One use of leftover wax that is an exciting challenge is appliqué, to go on previously made candles. You can cut many designs from puddles of wax while the wax is still warm and pliable. At this time the wax will adhere to the candle more willingly than later when the pieces are cold and rigid.

You can make small flower appliqués by using a demitasse or doll spoon. Grease the bowl of the spoon well and remove only one spoonful of wax from your vat at a time. Rest the bottom of the spoon, filled with the still fluid wax, on an ice cube for a moment. As soon as the bottom wax becomes opaque press the top surface of the wax in the spoon against the candle. A pattern of teardrops or petals can be created in this way. Pull and turn the smaller end of the teardrop with your fingers and you have a paisley pattern.

Daisies and similar flowers usually have an uneven number of petals. To make a well-designed 5-petal flower, place 1 petal for the "head," 2 for feet, and 2 more for arms. The petals needn't be equidistant; they aren't always perfectly spaced on a real flower. If you have extra-large spaces between petals, fill them in with other petals. If you get the proper balance, the flower will look fine.

Making stems can teach you another skill. Buy a small ear syringe. It need only hold 1 ounce of fluid but it must hold hot fluid. Some doll-nursing bottles will also work, but many will melt with the heat of the wax.

Practice squeezing water from your container in a controlled stream. When you can control the water it will be time to try wax. Be sure the water is totally removed from the container since it could distort the wax flow. You can practice on old newspapers, but if you use the bottom of a cake or pie pan, a piece of waxed paper or foil, or anything else with a smooth surface, you can reclaim your wax.

The hotter the wax the faster it will flow from your syringe. When you can control it in a steady stream, put the stem on your flower.

Don't burn your fingers. There is no reason not to wear gloves if you are more comfortable in them.

Stems and tendrils are sometimes made of string or crochet thread soaked in hot wax and then fastened to the candle. You can make tendrils by winding 1 or 2 inches of wax-dipped string over your finger. If you'd like many tendrils or a chain, wind the string over a lead pencil or piece of doweling. When the wax cools you can cut off the lengths you need for tendrils, or slash the entire length of coil and link the circlets together to form a chain.

Leaves and stems are sometimes added in a way that gives an impressionistic effect. Stir the thickening wax in a cooling vat and spoon this over the area that is to serve as a background for your flower. Imbed the flower while the wax is still hot and semi-fluid.

Use a pointed object to draw through the thick wax to make a stem or push the wax into leaf and stem shapes.

When you have mastered stems and leaves by this method, you can try a whole landscape. Waterfalls can be fun to make with this mode of decorating. You can also write messages or put all-over patterns on candles in this way.

11

The $20.00 Professional

There comes a day in the life of most hobby craftsmen when they need to be recognized as professionals. Somehow you outgrow the label of "hobbyist." You look around for ways to expand your horizons.

You have been designing and creating candles for a period of time. Your friends and relatives have probably flattered you by joyfully accepting all the handmade candles you would give them. Suddenly they are returning, sometimes with their friends, to ask for more—and more—and more.

How commercial your professional candle life becomes will be a matter of available time and economic and emotional need. Some people need major income; some people want only pin money, satisfaction, and expanded horizons. If you fall into the latter group, keep the first group in mind and never undersell yourself, or your product, just because you don't happen to need money at the moment.

Craftsmen who become professionals for an emotional or social satisfaction are frequently unrealistic about money. This is not only unfair to the craftsman who needs income but it is also self-destructive, since it downgrades the craftsman's own creativity.

It is always important to be aware of the price you pay for supplies. It is also important to know how much money and time you invest in each candle creation. As a hobbyist this information may only provide self-satisfaction. When you consider selling your very first candle, it becomes vitally important.

Any candle sold any time should always have a price tag larger than the sum of the raw materials.

Your labor should also be considered. Wages are considered so important that the United States government establishes a minimum wage for the most unskilled laborer. A candlemaker is *not* an unskilled laborer. What you add for labor costs depends on the value you personally place on your skill. You have every right to treat your skill with respect, and you short-change all other craftsmen when you don't.

You may not realize it, but starting a candle business will be an entire new area of learning for you. Think in terms of the least possible labor and the greatest profit potential. You will find it difficult, in the beginning, to pay yourself for your own labor. There will be many places you can't foresee where you will lose time, labor, or money. Don't get excited about the overall picture for at least a year. In this time you will gain some valuable experience.

Unless you are fully versed in the gift shop or interior decorating business, there are probably some idiosyncrasies you need to learn about the business outlets most likely to sell your product.

What you are offering are handcrafted, handmade, or hand-decorated candles—probably all three. Select the candles that you've enjoyed making most, the candles that have been most popular with others, and the candles that are most effective with the least labor.

Study these candles so you know exactly how much the raw materials cost and exactly how much time is involved in creating them. Search for faster, more efficient methods. Labor, today, is a major concern for everyone. Time is respected as money in a way it never was before. You must pay yourself for your time and you must show yourself a profit or your business will not be able to grow. Don't overlook the time you spend in all directions: candle-making, record-keeping and bookkeeping, shopping for supplies, and sales time.

Most small businesses operate at a loss for a time, but they thrive if the price is right, the product is right, and there is grow-room in the original thinking. Think ahead about everything possible that could affect you, even to how you'll pay wages if the need arises. Keep this in mind when you put a price on your product. Study the prices on other handcrafted candles. Don't price your candles out of your market.

Test your product for its acceptability to its customers by entering some of the local crafts shows operated by church and fraternal organizations. These will allow you to deal directly with your public. You will know if the public feels your prices are right, if the candles please them, and if the candle decorations are sturdy enough to hold up under shoppers' handling. Evaluate this information. Consider that the segment of the population that attended this particular show may not be the market you are trying to reach with your candles.

There may be real candle enthusiasts at the show and they may buy out all the candles you have brought. This is how you want things to go, but be sure to make note of which candles sold first while a complete selection was still available—never trust your memory on a business project. These may be the candles to specialize in for this particular community.

If the crafts show attendance is oriented toward do-it-yourself projects, you may be asked to teach candle-making. If you have the inclination and the classroom space, this can be a very rewarding enterprise.

Decide on how many students you can work with at one time. Usually five to ten are plenty. Are you going to teach candle-pouring or candle-decorating? (I'd recommend the latter for your first class.) What are other local craftsmen charging for classes? Don't underprice your teaching. Establish a price for the supplies the students need to purchase from you.

Make arrangements to purchase classroom supplies wholesale. Resell to your students at retail prices. This is part of the income professionals expect from their teaching.

When you are familiar with your buying market and with production methods you may desire to eliminate some personal selling and have your candles sold in retail shops. Don't attempt this until you fully comprehend your product potential.

Selecting the right shops is of primary importance. Your candles will probably cost more than commercial candles, and they should, since they are handmade and designed specifically for the community in which you sell them.

Select shops that feature one-of-a-kind, handcrafted items. Don't try for large volume sales. The shop that orders a gross today may want a gross on rush order next week, and you probably have no facilities to produce so much so quickly. Most of the one-of-a-kind shops will want no more than a dozen

Teach candle-making if you can. There is no other place in a professional's experience where success can be so rewarding. These are third-graders from Mrs. Read's class at the Bayberry School in Watchung, New Jersey, having their first lesson. (Photo by Joe De Caro)

of one kind; they may not want even that many. They will need to double the price they pay you in order to cover their expenses. A 100 percent mark-up is to be expected, since the shopkeeper has many overhead expenses to meet. If you find more than a 200 percent mark-up on the price paid you, it is time to renegotiate your contract with that shop.

You can afford to cut your retail price for a wholesale order, since you are eliminating the selling labor you charged for in your original price. Once a shop has established a price on a specific candle, don't ever sell that candle at a lower price to your own retail customers.

The following lists the equipment and supplies you will probably need to go into business for yourself. You needn't limit yourself to $20.00 if you have other funds available, but beware of overspending. Unless your need for cash return is extremely great and you have a reservoir of related experience you will learn far more—and build a more lasting business—if you start small and study your growth pattern.

List #1—Equipment

glass jar with tight-fitting top	small steady table
hot plate or stove	sharp knife
cookie sheet with four raised rims	hot pads

List #2—Supplies

paraffin	crayons	table salt
stearic acid	string or wicking	borax
other waxes		waxed paper or foil

List #3—Office Supplies

rubber stamp	labels	plastic wrap
stamp pad	cellophane tape	invoices
envelopes	writing paper	business cards (blank)
	record book	

Add to your equipment whatever you have used as a hobbyist. Your supplies will need the addition of specific materials to create whatever is your specialty. If you happen to prefer decorating tapers rather than making your own, you need to buy a good grade of commercial taper. It will guarantee a trouble-free base candle and eliminate much labor. Start looking for sources of quality supplies that are less expensive than those you have been using.

Your office materials can be extremely simple to begin with. Your customers won't mind your doing business with homemade business forms, provided your business is efficiently run.

A well-designed, carefully thought-out rubber stamp (business-card size) can be used on letterheads, business cards, invoices, return address labels, and for the return address on envelopes. You might like to use colored, rough-textured paper with torn edges or a colored stamp pad, rather than the customary black ink on white paper.

May I be the first to wish you prosperity.

Glossary

blended wax: wax formulated properly to accomplish a given objective

candle's shell, candle shell, shell candle: a hollow shell of wax—the outer decorated, detached section that surrounds a smaller, wicked candle. For example: hurricane chimneys of wax or a Christmas chimney candle

cast: the act of pouring wax into a form to create a candle

casting: the product of a mold. You cast a candle in a mold. The candle becomes the casting.

chandler: a candlemaker

coat: one layer of wax

color coat: the layer of wax that colors the candle

core wax: the wax in the center of the candle, specially formulated to burn well

crafted: the process of making candles that are neither poured nor dipped

cure: to allow a candle or a candlewick to sit for a period of time, to insure that all of the chemical ingredients have evaporated or cooled and the wax is cold and hard

dip: one plunge of the wick (plus whatever wax is already attached to it) into the wax vat, for the purpose of acquiring more wax on the wick or more girth for the candle

dip rack, dipping rack: also referred to as a wick dip; a specially designed tool to allow more than one candle to be dipped at a time. A dip rack might be larger than a wick dip, but the design would be similar.

feathering: The colonial dame feathered her candle by plunging it into very hot water, holding it by either the wick or the base, and shaking it vigorously until it was dry. This was to make the candle burn more evenly. The modern candlemaker sometimes uses the same technique to intermingle two colored waxes into a pattern.

Glossary | 125

flat wick: a braided wick. Braid is flat in comparison to a twist of string or rag or a narrow length of hide formerly used for a wick.

guttering: melted wax running down the outside of a candle when it is not a part of the candle design

layer: one consistent thickness of wax poured at one time and a part of the total candle

mold: any number of forms salvaged and/or manufactured, used to create a candle of a specific shape; also sometimes used to create decorations or relief motifs

paraffin: the most popular base wax used in candle-making

pour: to cast a candle using a mold

salts: chemical form of minerals added to color the flame of the candle, such as copper for turquoise, barium for shades of blue, and strontium for shades of red

sculpt or sculpture: fine art techniques applied to candles

shape: the silhouette of the candle

shape coat: the layer of wax specifically formulated to hold the candle shape in warm weather or while the candle burns. This is a formula designed to take more heat than the rest of the candle and usually comprises one layer of wax between the core of the candle and the candle decorations or color coat.

shrinkage cavity, shrinkage well: the hole left in the center of wax masses after the fluid wax has cooled and settled. As the wax cools it adheres to the outside of the candle and shrinks, creating a center hole.

snuffing: the process of removing wick ash and putting the candle out. In colonial days an accomplished snuffer could remove the ash without putting the candle out.

socket: the bottom end of the candle that fits into the candlestick

socket-well: the portion of the candlestick designed to receive the candle socket

soft candle: an uncured candle; a raw candle; a very fresh candle possibly still warm from vat; a candle not completely hardened or cooled

sprigging: small designs created separately and added to candle surface for decor

stearic acid: purified, stabilized form of tallow

tallow: fuel from animal fat; animal grease to be used for candle wax

vat: any container used to melt, formulate, or hold wax

votive candle, votive light, warmer candle: any small chunky candle that can be used for heat or light inside a candle shell, frequently fragranced and colored, but rarely decorated

wick dip: see *dip rack*. A wick dip is similar but is used only for dressing wicks.

wick dressing: the wax added to the wick before the wick is inserted in the candle

wicking: soft cotton or linen threads, string, or yarn, braided and soaked in special solution to be made into heart of candle

wick wax: core wax sometimes treated with fragrance or some other special property to give the candle a special burning feature

wick wire: tool specially made of strong wire. One end is heated to bore a hole in an otherwise finished candle so wick can be inserted. Ice picks are frequently used to put holes in smaller candles.

Index

Aging
   of candles, 3, 15-16, 124
   of wicks, 3, 16
Appliqués, 116-117

Ball-shaped candles, 74-75
Bayberry, 7, 8, 11, 12, 13
   cleaning, 19
   preparing, 20-21
Beeswax, 7, 8, 11, 12, 13
   cleaning, 18-20
Blended wax, 124
Borax, use on wicks, 32, 37
Boric acid, use on wicks, 32, 37
Bottles, use as molds, 69-71
Bunsen burner, 3
"Burning bushes," 101-103

Café candles, 91
Candelilla wax, 9
"Candle power," 8
Candleberry, 7
   preparing, 20-21
Candle-making
   classes in, 120, 121
   history of, 2-3
   problems involved, 16-17, 36-37

Candles
   professional, 118-123
   aging of, 3, 15-16, 124
   ball-shaped, 74-75
   bottle, 69-71
   café, 91
   ceremonial, 7
   chimney, 61, 62, 124
   color and, 38-46
   color coat on, 15-16, 53, 55, 124
   construction of, 11-12
   crafted, 125
   definition of (Webster's), 2
   design of, 46-47, 63-64, 85-91, 92-117
   dipped, 11, 14-15, 79-91
   fireplace, 111
   floating, 94-96
   flower, 93, 94, 95, 96
   graduated stacked, 110-111
   hanging, 76-78
   layered, 11, 12, 13
   molded, 50-78
   multicolored ornate, 66
   mushroom, 107, between pp. 52-53
   patio, 6
   poured, 11, 50-78
   religious, 7

Candles (*Continued*)
  round, 71
  sand-cast, 106-110
  sandwich, 99-101
  scented, 48-49
  sculptured, 11, 12, 112, 125, between pp. 52-53
  shape coat on, 15, 53, 79, 125
  shape of, 125
  shell, 124
  soft, 125
  sphere-shaped, 71-73
  tall, between pp. 52-53
  twisted, 97-99, between pp. 52-53
  uses for, 6, 7, 9-10, 96
  votive, 75, 76, 125
  "wick," 77
Cans, tin, use as molds, 62-63
Carnauba wax, 9
Cast, defined, 124
Casting
  definition of, 124
  sand, 106-110
Ceremonial candles, 7
Cerin wax, 9
Cerosin, 7
Cetin, 8
Chandler, defined, 124
Chimney candles, 61, 62, 124
Chinese wax, 9
Classes, candle-making, 120, 121
Cleaning, wax, 18-21
Coat
  color, 15-16, 53, 55, 124
  definition of, 124
  shape, 15, 53, 79, 125
Color, 38-46
  flame, 38-40
  formulas, 43-44
  testing of, 41
  wax, 40-46
Color coat, 15-16, 53, 55, 124
Cone-shaped cups, use as molds, 59-60

Construction, candle, 11-12
Core wax, definition of, 124
Crafted candles, 92-117, 124
Crafting, 92-117
Cups, cone-shaped, use as molds, 59-60
Cure, *see* Aging
Cylinders, dipping of, 81

Decorating, equipment for, 30
Decorations, reviving, 112
Design, candle, 46-47, 63-64, 85-91, 92-117
Dip, defined, 124
Dpped candles, 11, 14-15, 79-91
Dipping, 11, 14-15
  equipment for, 28, 29
  techniques, 79-91
Dipping rack, 28, 80, 81, 82, 83
  cleaning, 81
  defined, 124
Doughnuts, 96, 97

Equipment, 25-30, 122-123
  decorating, 30
  dipping, 28, 29

Feathering, 79, 124
Fireplace candles, 111
Flame, candle, 35-36
  color of, 38-40
Flat wick, 125
Floating candles, 94-96
Flower candles, 93, 94, 95, 96
Flowers, artificial, reviving, 112
Formulas
  color, 43-44
  flame color, 39
  wax, 12-13, 79
Fragrances, 48-49
Froth, wax, 61, 103-106

Glass molds, 57, 69-71, 113-115
Graduated stacked candles, 110-111

Granules, wax, 115-116
Guttering, 36, 125

Hanging candles, 76-78
History, candle-making, 2-3
Hobnail patterns, 112

Indians, American, candles made by, 2

Japan wax, 9

Kitchen molds, 66

Lanolin, 9
Layer, defined, 125
Layered candles, 11, 12, 13
Leftovers, using, 113-117
Licuri, 9

Marketing, 118-122
Milk cartons, use as molds, 57-58
Mineral wax, 9
Molded candles, 50-78
Molds, 30, 31, 50-77, 125
  bottles used as, 69-71
  commercial, 50, between pp. 52-53
  glass, 57, 69-71, 113-115
  kinds of, 50
  kitchen, 66
  paper, 57-62
  squeaky-toy, 68-69
  tin can, 62-63
Montan wax, 9
Mushroom candles, 107, between pp. 52-53
Myrtleberry, 7, 8
  preparing, 20-21

Notebooks, use of, 3, 4

Office suppiles, 122, 123
Ouricury, 9
Ozocerites, purified, 9

Paper molds, 57-62
Paraffin, 6-7, 8, 10, 12, 13, 15, 79, 125
Patio candles, 6
Pilgrims, wax used by, 8
Polka dots, 88
Pour, defined, 125
Poured candles, 11, 50-78
Prices, candle, 118-122
Problems, candle-making, 16-17, 36-37
Professional candle-makers, 118-123

Racks, dipping, *see* Dipping racks
Reclaiming, wax, 21-23
Religious candles, 7
Round candles, 71

Salts, 125
Sand-cast candles, 106-110
Sandwich candles, 99-101
Sawhorses, small, making, 88, 89
Sealing wax, 9
Scented candles, 48-49
Sculptured candles, 11, 12, 112, 125, between pp. 52-53
Selling, 118-122
Shape, defined, 125
Shape coat, 15, 53, 79, 125
Sheet wax, 92
Shell candle, 124
Shrinkage well, 11, 12, 125
Snuffing, 125
Socket, defined, 125
Socket-well, 125
Soft candles, 125
Sphere-shaped candles, 71-73
Spermaceti, 8
Sprigging, 125
Stacked candles, 110-111
Stearic acid, 8, 9, 11, 12, 13, 15, 79, 125
Sterin, 8
Storage, wax, 24
Suet, as source of tallow, 20

Supplies, 122, 123
Swimming pools, candles for, 96
Synthetic waxes, 9

Tall candles, between pp. 52-53
Tallow, 9, 125
   cleaning, 20
   source of, 20
Tapers
   dipping, 80, 81
   variations in treatment of, between pp. 52-53
Teaching, 120, 121
Texture, 63-66
Thermometer, use of, 6, 10
Thomforde, Betty, between pp. 52-53
Tin cans, use as molds, 62-63
Toys, use as molds, 68-69
Tubes, paper, use as molds, 58-59
Twisted candles, 97-99

Vats, 27
   defined, 125
Votive candles, 75, 76, 125

Waxes, 5-24
   amount needed, 13
   base, 6-9
   blended, 124
   borax or boric acid treatment of, 32, 37
   cleaning, 18-21
   color and, 40-46
   formula, 12-13, 79
   inflammability of, 5
   preformulated, 7
   removal of, if spilled on self, 5
   selecting, 6-10
   storing, 24
   synthetic, 126
   used, reclaiming, 21-23
"Wick" candles, 77
Wick dip, *see* Dipping rack
Wick dressing, 126
Wick wax, 126
Wick wire, 126
Wicking, 126
Wicks, 32-37
   aging of, 3, 16
   materials used for, 32, 33, 126
   preparation of, 33, 35
   problems involving, 36-37
   size of, 33
Wire, wick, 126
Workshop, 25-26

```
745.59  Chisholm, K.     589212
C  H      Lomneth

          The candlemaker's
           primer
```

DATE			
MAY 30 '72			
SEP 19 '74			
NOV 13 '74			
APR 27 1976			
OCT 1 1976			
SEP 25 1978			
1 8			

Piscataway, New Jersey

St. Mary Regional High School
Library
310 Augusta Street
South Amboy, New Jersey 08879

© THE BAKER & TAYLOR CO.